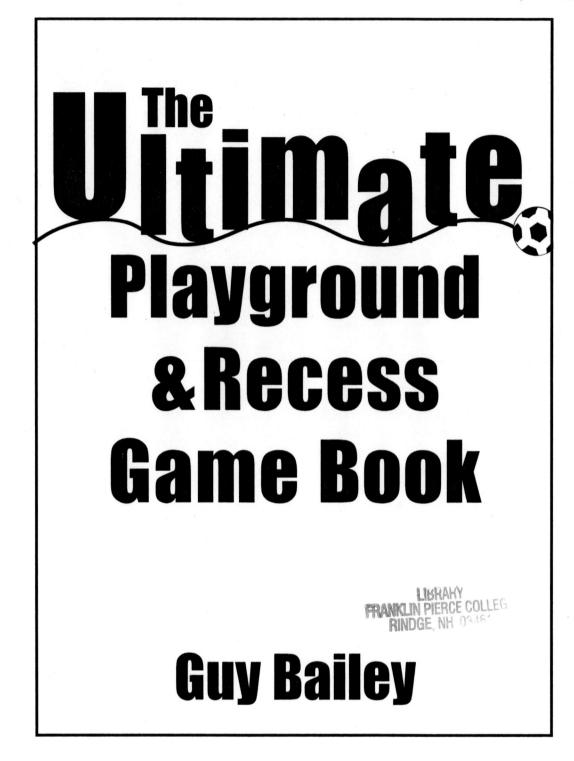

The Ultimate Playground & Recess Game Book

Guy Bailey

Educators Press

Copyright © 2001 by
EDUCATORS PRESS

ISBN: 0-9669727-2-4

Publisher's Cataloging-in-Publication
(Provided by Quality Books,Inc.)

Bailey, Guy , 1956-
        The ultimate playground & recess game book /
Guy Bailey ; illustrated by Cynthia Wilson.-- 1st
ed.
        p. cm.
        Includes index.
        LCCN: 00-190754
        ISBN: 0-9669727-2-4

        1. Games. 2. Playgrounds. 3. Recesses.
4. Sports for children. 5. Play. I. Title.

CURR   GV1201 B35 2001   796.1
                                                    QBIOO-504

EDUCATORS PRESS
5333 NW Jackson St.
Camas, WA 98607
(360) 834-3049

Printed in the United States by
Morris Publishing
3212 East Highway 30
Kearney, NE 68847
1-800-650-7888

Acknowledgements

As any author will tell you, the first person to experience sacrifice in the writing of a book is the author's spouse. I could never say enough "thanks" to my wife, Shelby, for putting up with the many hours apart from me as I worked at my computer, and the many hours she has worked herself on the production of this book. I am truly blessed to have such a talented, inspiring, and loving person in my life.

I would also like to give thanks to my "work family" : the staff and students at Mill Plain Elementary School in Vancouver, Washington. For the past 13 years, my friends there have made going to work a truly meaningful and fun experience. I have benefited and learned so very much about teaching, and about life, in my relationship with them all.

I am particularly indebted to Cynthia Wilson of Vancouver, Washington, for her masterful illustrations and her talent at book formatting. The teaching and understanding of these games is made much easier because of her contributions. As in my previous book, *The Ultimate Sport Lead-Up Game Book*, Cynthia has a special artistic gift for making games come " alive" for readers.

I also would like to acknowledge the professionals at Morris Publishing, the company that did the printing and cover design of this book. Their professionalism and dedicated focus on producing a quality product is very much appreciated. Their staff's friendliness and courteous way of conducting business made the final phase of producing this book the easiest part of the journey—thanks!

A WORD FROM THE AUTHOR

Books are teachers. Good books go right on instructing in odd moments when the teachers and parents are not on duty.

Anonymous

...and that's my hope and desire for this book. When young people are offered meaningful play experiences, they discover the pleasures of moving and playing for self-discovery, fun, and fitness enhancement. The interest that children develop from these activities today can influence their behavior for a lifetime.

In my previous book, *The Ultimate Sport Lead-Up Game Book*, I wrote about the necessity for using learning activities that are fun and meaningful. Students learn when they are inspired and motivated by teachers who make learning fun. Our classrooms, gymnasiums, and playgrounds should be places where learning becomes play and play becomes learning.

My desire for you is that these carefully selected games will help you launch a lifetime of moving, learning, and fun with your students – that they keep on playing and developing their physical and life skills "when the teachers and parents are not on duty," motivated forever because of what happened on the school playground.

I hope you find *The Ultimate Playground & Recess Game Book* a useful resource and a good "teacher."

The real joy of life is in its play. Play is anything we do for the joy and love of doing it. It is the real living of life with the feeling of freedom and self-expression. It is the business of childhood, and its continuation in later years is the prolongation of youth.

Walter Rauschenbusch

PREFACE

This book was written to solve the long-desired need for a playground and recess game resource that would help create a safe, healthy, and peaceful playground setting for our children. Many school professionals will tell you that recess behavioral problems are often the result of student boredom. As one who has worked with kids for over 20 years, I would concur. *The Ultimate Playground & Recess Game Book* addresses this problem through the use of fun and meaningful games for children. The material offered here will help you provide a quality and invigorating recess experience for your students.

I expect *The Ultimate Playground & Recess Game Book* to appeal to school professionals such as classroom teachers, physical educators, and playground supervisors, as well as camp directors, recreational instructors and parents. Anyone who has faced the challenge of presenting meaningful playground and recess activities to students will find a treasure of exciting and useful ideas here. The usage of these games is unlimited and can serve teachers and game instructors in a variety of diverse situations.

The Ultimate Playground & Recess Game Book meets the need for student fun and variety by offering over 170 games and sport activities. The games themselves incorporate a wide range of interests and skill proficiency from traditional tried-and-true favorites (as in hopscotch) to sport lead-up games (like No-Team Softball). There are game ideas for large groups as well as small groups; games for outside grassy areas, as well as pavement; games for use in the gymnasium; and rainy-day classroom activities.

These games can be used on an informal basis as in recess, or as a planned and integral part of the physical education curriculum. Each game comes with complete, easy-to-read directions, instructional suggestions, and scoring procedures. An illustration accompanies many of these games to help you visualize the set-up and directions. Also included is a convenient activity finder chart that makes it a cinch to games suitable for a child's grade level.

The significance of playground games and sports in a child's physical, social, and emotional development cannot be overstated. Anyone who regularly spends time around kids will soon realize that they play to learn more about themselves and the world around them. In many ways, the playground experience is a laboratory of life. By helping individual games come alive for children and individual children come alive through game playing, this resource can contribute to a quality recess experience for children during this important part of their daily life.

It is the child in man that is the source of his uniqueness and creativeness, and the playground is the optimal milieu for the unfolding of his capaciities and talents.

Eric Hoffer, (1902-83), philosopher

CONTENTS

Chapter Four　　　　　*Relay Games*　　　　　*99*

Chapter Five　　　*Classroom Games & Activities*　　　*113*

Chapter Six　　　*Games Using Ropes, Hoops & Other Fun Stuff !*　　　*129*

The Role Of Elementary School Recess & Games

There exists an erroneous belief among many that the school recess serves no real educational purpose and that recess is just children" playing" with no real learning taking place. Nothing, however, could be further from the truth. The roles of recess and games are vital to a child's overall healthy development. In fact, recess is one of the most significant learning experiences that a child will encounter on the road to adulthood. The many educational benefits of recess and game playing include:

◆ Game playing teaches us the "rules of life." As youngsters ourselves at one time, we can remember how games taught us to work together and how to help others. Through games, children can act out real-life situations. They learn how to solve problems, look for alternatives, and resolve arguments. Recess activities like tetherball, four square and hopscotch encourage children to take turns and act cooperatively with each other. By following the rules of a game, children learn how to work within defined guidelines and to accept the consequences if they do not. By experiencing these situations as children, they accumulate life-skills that will prove to be invaluable during their later years when they must deal with work and adult relationships.

◆ Through play, children can create a safe setting in which to test their minds and their physical capabilities. At their own pace, they can experiment with building relationships of the same and opposite gender, to feel what it's like to be a leader or a follower, to teach others or be taught, to play right field or be the pitcher, to chase or be chased, to win and to lose. Game playing offers children the opportunities to master these mental and physical obstacles that keep changing as their minds and bodies mature.

◆ Children also get to experience the real world by losing or winning at games. This "win some, lose some" reality of life begins when they play their first game. Since most games have winning as an objective, children learn how to accept positive and negative outcomes. Through play, they learn about healthy competition and how effort, persistence, and determination can affect the outcome of a game. By offering a wide variety of recess games, game leaders can be guaranteed of at least one sport or activity where a child can experience personal success. This presents opportunities for children to build confidence and enhances self-image.

◆ The opportunity to play with friends is a motivating reason for many children, regardless of age, to come to school. As a consequence, recess is often the favorite part of the school day for many students. This is especially true in rural areas or harsh climate areas where the chance to interact socially with others is limited. Recess allows children the time and setting

(continued on next page)

to build friendships. Additionally, it provides a time to learn how to relate to other children from various ethnic and social-economic backgrounds. Recess and game playing allows this cultural exchange to happen in a non-threatening environment.

♦ In addition to all the social, emotional, and cognitive benefits, game playing affords an avenue for healthy physical exercise. Recently, there has been an increased concern regarding the health and fitness level of children. The lifestyles of too many children include excessive television viewing, sitting at the computer, and junk food. Time formerly spent playing active games with neighborhood friends is being spent at more sedentary activities. Recent studies have shown a higher percentage of overweight children than ever previously recorded. This change in lifestyle has produced a nation of unfit children, many of whom are already saddled with significant cardiac risk factors. Many of today's young people are unaware of the necessity to be physically fit, and they lack either the knowledge and/or the motivation to improve. Recess and the use of playground games gives school professionals a daily window of time to reverse this alarming trend and to initiate healthful changes in young people that will enrich their lives.

♦ A direct correlation exists between exercise and classroom performance. Recent studies show that children who participate in daily physical activities function at a higher level intellectually than those who do not. When children are deprived of vigorous physical activity, the heart isn't given the opportunity to pump fresh oxygen into the blood to nourish and stimulate the brain. Recess allows valuable time in the school day for children to participate in fitness enhancing activities.

As school professionals, game leaders, and parents, we have the opportunity to make the playground a significant learning experience for children. Besides physical education (which unfortunately is not offered in all of our nation's elementary and middle schools on a daily basis), no other school setting has more potential for emotional, social, cognitive, and physical growth development than the playground. The participation in playground activities that children experience today can influence their behavior for a lifetime.

How To Use This Book

The Ultimate Playground & Recess Game Book is divided into six sections: traditional playground games, sports and sport lead-up games, large & small group games, relay games, classroom games, and mixed games using equipment. Traditional playground games include many of the tried and true favorites such as Four Square and Tetherball. The sport category includes team and lifetime sport activities. Large and small group games include low-organized, tag, and cooperative activities. Relay games include those that can played with various sized groups. Classroom games are included for those rainy day situations that require recess to be held indoors. The equipment-based mixed game section includes jump rope, hula hoop, and manipulative activities that all children enjoy playing.

The Activity Finder is designed to help you locate games and activities quickly and easily. The activities are listed alphabetically. Each activity is given a suggested grade level range, the category under which it fits (traditional, sport, group game, relay, classroom, mixed), where the game can be played (outside, gymnasium, classroom), and the page number where the game can be found.

Here are a few safety guidelines and game selection tips before implementing these games with your students.

- For student enjoyment and success, the games selected for use should be suitable to student skills and ages and organized for maximum participation.
- Playground leaders should adapt and modify games in whatever ways necessary to meet the needs and abilities of the students and to make maximum use of the space and time available.
- Game leaders should discuss safety precautions before the playing of all new games.
- The playground should be free of obstacles and any potentially hazardous objects.
- All recess games should be properly supervised.
- Proper use of playground equipment should be taught at the beginning of each school year.
- Students should wear tennis shoes when participating in games.

* Please note that the term he and him are used throughout this book to represent both genders equally.

ACTIVITY FINDER

Game Category

KEY		
	T = Traditional	R = Relay
	S = Sport/Sport Lead-Up	C = Classroom
	G = Large Group	M = Ropes, Hoops, Misc.

	Suggested Grade Levels	Game Category	Outside	Gym	Classroom	Page
			WHERE TO PLAY			
Add 'Em Up	3-6	S (Softball)	X			68
Alphabetical Numbers	1-6	C			X	114
Animal Tag	K-3	G	X	X		93
Answer Scramble	K-8	C			X	114
Around the World-Basketball	3-8	S (Basketball)	X	X		38
Around The World-Four Square	2-8	T	X			22
Back To Back	K-6	C	X	X		115
Badminton	3-8	S (Badminton)	X	X		34
Balloon Volleyball	1-8	C			X	116
Bamboozle "Em	K-3	G	X	X		76
Baserunning Relay	2-8	R	X			102
Basketball Pirates	2-6	S (Basketball)	X	X		43
Battle-Four Square	2-8	T	X			22
Beachball Volleyball	3-8	S (Volleyball)	X	X		70
Beanbag Four Square	3-8	T	X			21
Beanbag Horseshoes	2-8	T	X	X		130
Beanbag Relay	K-8	R	X	X		103
Beanbag Relay-Indoor	K-6	C			X	116
Beanbag Tag	K-6	G	X	X		93
Blob Tag	K-6	G	X	X		91
Bocce Croquet	2-8	M	X			132
Bridge Tag	K-6	G	X	X		92
Bull In The Ring	2-8	S (Basketball)	X	X		42
Caboose Tag	K-6	G	X	X		95
Capture The Flag	3-8	G	X			77
Capture The Footballs	3-8	S (Football)	X			47
Catch 22	3-6	S (Volleyball)	X	X		72
Charades	3-8	C			X	117
Chariots Of Fire Relay	1-8	R	X	X		105
Circle Soccer	K-6	S (Soccer)	X	X		61
Circle Tag	K-6	G	X	X		94
Clean The Chute-Parachute	K-6	M	X	X		139
Continuous Passing Relay	2-8	R	X	X		102
Crab Soccer	K-6	S (Soccer)	X	X		58
Cricket Ball	2-8	S (Cricket)	X			44
Croquet	2-8	M	X			130
Cross Country Relay	1-8	R	X			104
Crows And Cranes	K-4	G	X		X	78

	Suggested Grade Levels	Game Category	Outside	Gymnasium	Classroom	Page
Doctor Dodgeball	1-6	G	X		X	78
Dome-Parachute	K-6	M	X		X	140
Doubles Four Square	2-8	T	X			22
Dribble & Hop Relay	2-8	R	X	X		100
Dribble Freeze Tag	K-6	S (Soccer)	X	X		61
Dribble, Pivot & Pass	3-8	R	X	X		101
Elbow Tag	K-6	G	X	X		92
End Ball	3-8	G	X	X		79
End Zone	3-8	S (Football)	X	X		48
Everyone's It	K-6	G	X	X		94
Fake 'em Out	3-8	S (Football)	X	X		49
Five Catches	3-6	S (Football)	X	X		50
Flickerball	3-8	G	X			80
Four Ball Shootout	3-8	S (Soccer)	X			60
Four Square	2-8	T	X			20
Four Square Volleyball	3-8	S (Volletball)	X	X		73
Frisbee Golf	3-8	S (Golf)	X			50
Germ Tag	K-6	G	X	X		94
Getting Warmer & Colder	K-3	C			X	118
Gotcha	2-6	S (Basketball)	X	X		41
Half-Court Basketball	3-8	S (Basketball)	X	X		37
Handball	2-8	T	X	X		23
Hill Dill	K-4	G	X	X		81
Hit The Deck Tag	K-6	G	X	X		92
Home Run Football	3-8	S (Football)	X			46
Hopscotch	K-6	T	X			24
Horse	3-8	S (Basketball)	X	X		38
How Many Words	K-4	C			X	119
Hula Hoop Bumper Tag	K-6	M	X			134
Hula Hoop Challenges	K-6	M	X	X		133
Hula Hoop Circle Relay	K-8	M	X	X		135
Hula Hoop Relay	K-8	C	X	X	X	119
Igloo-Parachute	K-6	M	X	X		142
I Saw	K-6	C			X	118
Keep It Up	3-8	S (Volleyball)	X	X		70
Kickball	3-8	T	X			26
Kindergarten Four Square	K-1	T	X			21
King Square	3-8	T	X			28
Knock Out	3-8	S (Basketball)	X	X		40
Laugh Tag	K-4	G	X	X		93
Leap Frog Relay	K-6	R	X	X		107
Limbo	K-8	C		X	X	120
Line Tag	K-6	G	X	X		92
Little Brown Bear	K-2	G	X			82

(continued on next page)

Activity Finder (cont.)

	Suggested Grade Levels	Game Category	Outside	Gym	Classroom	Page
Long Base Kickball	2-6	T	X			27
Long Rope Challenges	K-8	M	X			135
Man From Mars	K-2	G	X	X		106
Mass Soccer	K-3	S (Soccer)	X			56
Mat Ball	3-8	G	X		X	83
Mathematical Baseball	1-8	C			X	120
Maypole	K-4	T	X			28
Merry Go Round-Parachute	K-4	M	X	X		141
Miniature Croquet Golf	2-8	M	X			129
Mini-Blob Tag	K-6	G	X	X		91
Mini-Team Handball	4-8	S	X	X		51
Modified Slo-Pitch	3-8	S (Softball)	X			65
Modified Soccer	K-6	S (Soccer)	X			56
Movement Skill Relays	K-6	R	X	X		106
Musical Chairs	K-6	C,G		X	X	121
Newcomb	3-6	S (Volleyball)	X	X		72
Non-Elimination Musical Chairs	K-6	C, G		X	X	122
Non-Elimination Simon Says	K-6	C,G	X	X	X	126
No-Net Badminton	3-8	S (Badminton)	X	X		35
No-Outs Kickball	2-8	T	X			27
No-Outs Softball	3-8	S (Softball)	X			65
North Wind-South Wind	K-6	G	X	X		93
No Rules Basketball	2-4	S (Basketball)	X	X		40
No Rules Volleyball	3-4	S (Volleyball)	X	X		71
No-Team Softball	3-8	S (Softball)	X			66
Number Exchange	K-6	M	X	X		141
One Chance Football	3-8	S (Football)	X			48
One Chance Softball	3-8	S (Softball)	X			68
Outside Field Billiards	3-8	S	X			52
Over 'N Under Relay	2-8	R	X	X		100
Paddle Ball-Four Square	3-8	T	X			21
Parachute Golf	2-8	M	X	X		144
Parachute Steal The Bacon	1-8	M	X	X		145
Parachute Volleyball	2-8	M	X	X		143
Partner Steal The Bacon	1-8	C		X	X	123
Partner Tag	K-6	G	X	X		95
Pass 'N Duck Relay	2-8	R	X	X		101
Pickle	3-8	S (Softball)	X			67
Pin Ball	2-8	G	X	X		84
Pin Soccer	1-8	S (Soccer)	X	X		62
Poisonous Snakes-Parachute	K-6	M	X	X		142
Pony Express	2-8	R	X			109
Popcorn-Parachute	K-6	M	X	X		139
Prisoners Dodgeball	2-8	G	X	X		85
Red Light-Green Light	K-2	G	X	X		86

	Suggested Grade Levels	Game Category	Outside	Gym	Classroom	Page
Regulation Basketball	3-8	S (Basketball)	X	X		36
Regulation Soccer	K-8	S Soccer)	X			54
Rescue Relay	K-6	R	X	X		110
Sack The Quarterback	2-6	G	X	X		87
Schoolroom Tag	K-3	C			X	123
Scoop Lacrosse	4-8	S (Lacrosse)	X			53
Sedan Relay	3-8	R	X	X		105
Shark-Parachute	K-6	M	X			143
Short Rope Challenges	K-8	M	X	X		146
Silent Ball	1-8	C			X	124
Simon Says	K-4	C,G	X	X	X	125
Soccer Bull	K-8	S (Soccer)	X			58
Soccer Croquet	2-8	S (Soccer)	X			59
Soccer Golf	2-8	S (Soccer)	X			59
Softball	3-8	S (Softball)	X			63
Sports Draw	2-6	C			X	126
Sports Tag	K-6	G	X	X		93
Spot Tag	K-6	G	X	X		95
Spud	2-6	G	X	X		87
Squat Tag	K-6	G	X	X		92
Squirrels In The Trees	K-3	G	X	X		88
Steal the Beanbags	3-8	G	X	X		89
Stuck In The Mud Tag	K-6	G	X	X		91
Sunday	K-3	G	X	X		96
Team Four Square	3-8	T	X			23
Team Three-On-Three	3-8	S (Basketball)	X	X		43
Team Tug-Of-War	1-8	M	X			149
Tetherball	2-8	T	X			29
3-On-3 Soccer	K-6	S (Soccer)	X			57
Three Team Softball	3-8	S (Softball)	X			64
Throw Softball	3-6	S (Softball)	X			66
Touch Football	3-8	S (Football)	X			45
Train Relay	2-8	R	X	X		107
Traveling Tasks Relay	K-8	R	X	X		111
Trees	K-4	G	X	X		96
Triple Play	3-8	S (Basketball)	X	X		41
Truth Or Consequences	1-6	G	X	X		30
Twenty-One	3-8	S (Basketball)	X	X		39
Two Square	1-8	T	X			30
Ultimate Frisbee	3-8	G	X			98
Volleyball	3-8	S (Volleyball)	X	X		69
Wall Ball	2-8	T	X	X		31
Wall Tunnel Tag	K-6	G		X		95
Wheelbarrow Relay	2-8	R	X			106
Where's My Mates	K-6	C	X	X	X	127
Who Has The Treasure	K-3	C			X	128

The true object of all human life is play. Earth is a task garden; heaven is a playground.

G. K. Chesterton (1874-1936), British author

CHAPTER ONE

TRADITIONAL PLAYGROUND GAMES

Most of our school and public playgrounds offer some combination of tetherball poles, four square, and hopscotch lines as built-in game possibilities for children. Many of the games contained in this chapter have been played by children for generations. These classic, easy-to-learn recess games are sure to offer lots of challenging fun for your students.

FOUR SQUARE

WHERE TO PLAY: Outside on pavement
NUMBER OF PLAYERS: 4 at one time
GRADE LEVELS: 2nd-8th grades
EQUIPMENT: One playground ball; chalk if necessary

HOW TO PLAY: Four Square is played very much like Two Square. However, Four Square utilizes a larger court and more players. The size of the court can range from 8' by 8' for the younger students to 16' by 16' for the upper elementary grades. The court consists of four equal squares, with each labeled A, B, C, and D. The server's square is normally marked off with a line drawn diagonally across the A square.

Before play begins, each of the players assumes a standing position in one of the four squares. The server (A) starts the game by bouncing the ball once behind the serving line and, with an open hand, bats it into one of the other squares. The player receiving the serve must let it bounce once before hitting it into another square. Play continues until a fault has been committed by one of the four players.

A fault is any one of the following: (1) stepping over the line while serving; (2) hitting a ball out of bounds; (3) hitting a line with the ball; (4) failing to return a hit made to your square; (5) or using an overhand throw or fist to hit the ball.

When a fault has occurred, the players shift positions. If the server (A) commits a fault, he moves to square D, D moves to C, C moves to B, and B becomes the next server. The objective is to move up a square after each fault and eventually become the server.

When playing with only four players, the one who committed a fault moves to square D and the others rotate to fill in empty squares. However, if a game has more than four players, the one who commits a fault leaves the court and joins the line of players waiting to get back into the game. A player from front of the line moves into square D and the other three players move up one square.

Four Square

One of the best things about Four Square is that there is no declared winner at the end. The players that make the fewest mistakes are simply rewarded with the greatest amount of playing time.

In addition to regular Four Square, there are many different variations of the game using the same court. Some of these include:

KINDERGARTEN FOUR SQUARE

In most cases, the five to seven year old child has not developed the agility or coordination to react and tap the ball as called for in regulation Four Square. This version allows the younger child to play with success by substituting catching and tossing instead of the normal serve and tap. Four square rules apply, except that each player catches the ball after the first bounce in his square and then underhand tosses it into another's square.

Play continues in this fashion throughout the game.

BEANBAG FOUR SQUARE

The game is played like regular four square (see rules), except that scoops and a bean bag are used instead of a playground ball. Player rotation stays the same.

A foul is committed when (1) the bean bag falls inside a player's square; (2) throwing the bean bag out of bounds; (3) throwing the bean bag so it hits on a line; (4) touching or throwing the bean bag with a leg or arm (anything other than a scoop); (5) having the bean bag fall out of the scoop; (6) and throwing with an overhand motion.

PADDLE BALL-FOUR SQUARE

This version of Four Square is played exactly like Beanbag Four Square (see above) above except that racquetball size paddles and tennis balls are used. Player rotation is the same as Four Square.

Paddle Ball-Four Square

(continued on next page)

Paddle Ball-Four Square (cont.)

A foul is committed when (1) a player allows a hit ball to land inside his square; (2) the ball is hit out of bounds; (3) the hit ball lands on a line; (4) and touching the ball with anything other than the paddle.

AROUND THE WORLD FOUR SQUARE

This fun variation has similar game rules of Four Square with one exception – the ball has to be hit in a certain direction. If the server serves to the right, the ball has to continue going around the square to the right. However, the server can yell "left" and change the direction anytime the ball lands in his square. Continue until someone commits a fault.

DOUBLES FOUR SQUARE

This is the same game of Four Square but with two players (partners) at each square with one in the square and the other waiting outside the square. As soon as the partner inside the square hits the ball, he quickly gets out and his partner (who is waiting outside the square) steps into the square prepared to hit the next ball. Partners continue this switching off throughout the game. Regular Four Square rules are used so if one partner commits a fault both partners go to the end of the waiting line. This is a great variation of Four Square for those times when the number of courts is limited.

Doubles Four Square

BATTLE FOUR SQUARE

Regulation Four Square rules apply unless the server calls out "Battle!" before serving. When this happens, the server can hit the ball to anyone, but the other players must always play the ball back to the server. This continues until a player misses or the server calls out "Battle's over!" When the "Battle's over" call is made, play resumes as regulation Four Square.

TEAM FOUR SQUARE

   Team Four Square is a bigger version of Doubles Four Square (see above). The squares need to be larger than those in regular Four Square--about 6' would be ideal. There can be 3-4 players in each square and, unlike Doubles Four Square, players stay inside their squares without alternating turns. The rules and fouls are the same as in regular Four Square. This is a great choice for those times when you have many students and you want to keep them actively involved.

HANDBALL

WHERE TO PLAY: Outside on a hard surface with a wall
NUMBER OF PLAYERS: 2 to 4 players at one time
GRADE LEVELS: 2nd-8th grades
EQUIPMENT: One tennis ball and a wall

HOW TO PLAY: A playing surface much as in Wall Ball is needed. Although a regulation handball court is 20' by 34', most elementary playgrounds will not have these markings. Chalk can be used to draw these lines, as well as the serving line which normally is 16' from the wall.

(continued on next page)

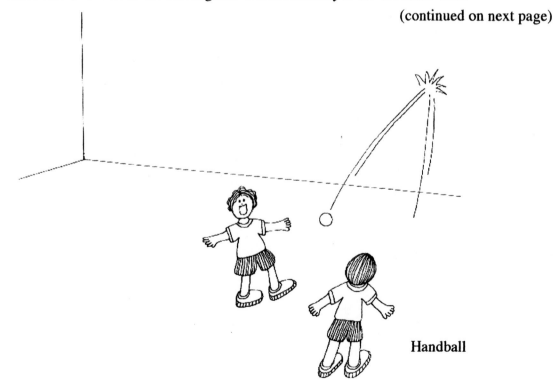

Handball

Handball (cont.)

The server starts the game by bouncing the ball on the ground and, as it comes up, hitting it at the wall. The ball must bounce back over the serving line to be considered legal. A server has two tries to make a legal serve. The opponent tries to hit the served ball back against the wall. The ball can be hit after it bounces or while still on the fly.

The players attempt to hit the ball back and forth continuously until one fails to hit it, or hits it out of bounds, or else hits it over the wall. If the server makes the mistake, the serve goes to the other player. If the player receiving the serve makes the error, the server is awarded a point. Players can only score points when they are serving.

The first player to score 21 points is the winner.

Doubles (2 players vs. 2 players) can also used with play being essentially the same. Only the partner closest to the ball returns it. Scoring is the same as in singles.

HOPSCOTCH

WHERE TO PLAY: On pavement
NUMBER OF PLAYERS: Any number
GRADE LEVELS: K-6 grades
EQUIPMENT: A diagram (see variations); chalk if necessary; an object for a marker

HOW TO PLAY: This is a classic game that has been played by children around the world for centuries. Although there are many different Hopscotch diagrams (see below), the objective is basically the same--to complete the course successfully without committing a foul.

For basic hopscotch (see diagram), the first player in line throws a marker into box #1. The player then hops on one foot to the end of the court, hopping over the square that contains the marker. This same player, once in the last box, turns and hops back again. He would stop at the second box, pick up the marker from the first box and hop out.

If this player has successfully completed his first turn without any fouls, he would then proceed to throwing the marker inside box #2 and so forth. Players should take turns, always starting where they left off, until someone has successfully navigated all the spaces.

Wherever there are two boxes side by side, a player can land with one foot in each block. Single boxes are hopped on one foot only.

A player forfeits a turn and must return to the back of the line whenever any of the following fouls have been committed: (1) failure to throw the marker fully inside the intended box; (2) stepping on a line; (3) hopping into a box that contains the marker; (4) using hands to support oneself while picking up a marker. The first player to complete the course successfully wins the game.

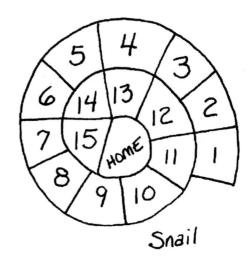

Snail

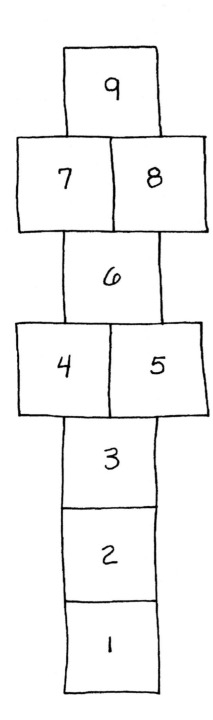

Basic

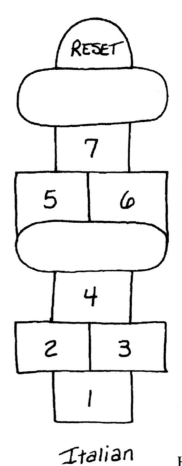

Italian

Hopscotch

KICKBALL

WHERE TO PLAY: Outdoors, preferably on a softball field
NUMBER OF PLAYERS: 6-9 on a team; two teams
GRADE LEVELS: 3rd-8th grades
EQUIPMENT: A large playground ball or foam soccer ball

HOW TO PLAY: First, form two equal teams. One team lines up to kick and the other team assumes fielding positions (as in softball). The game is played very much like softball with the following exceptions:

1) Instead of batting, a ball is rolled by the pitcher to the batter who kicks it. After the kick, the kicker runs the bases as in softball.

2) The fielding team can put the kicker out by catching a fly ball, tagging the runner while between bases, or forcing the runner out by getting the ball to a base before the runner gets there.

3) No leading-off or base stealing is allowed by the baserunners.

4) There are unlimited outs. Teams switch places after everyone on the kicking team has kicked. One point is scored each time the kicker has safely returned home. The team with the highest number of points (or "runs") at the end of a designated number of innings wins the game.

Kickball

NO-OUTS KICKBALL

This game is played in a setting much like regular softball but without the normal "outs." The objective for the kicker is to kick the ball out into fair territory and run the bases without stopping before the catcher gains possession of the ball and yells "freeze." This is the signal for the baserunner to stop running and to stay in that position, even if he is not on a base. When the next kicker kicks the ball, the baserunner(s) start running again around the bases until the next "freeze" signal. The baserunners do not stop after circling the bases once; they continue to run and score until everyone on their team has kicked. A point is scored each time a baserunner touches home base. Teams switch places when everyone has kicked.

LONG BASE KICKBALL

This is another version of kickball but it's played with only one base. Kickers can either run to the base and back, or stay on the base. Baserunners can stay on the base until there are three players; then, on the next kick, all the baserunners must run. Runners who successfully go to the base and touch home base score one point for their team. Teams switch places after everyone has had a chance to kick. Outs are made just as they are in regulation kickball.

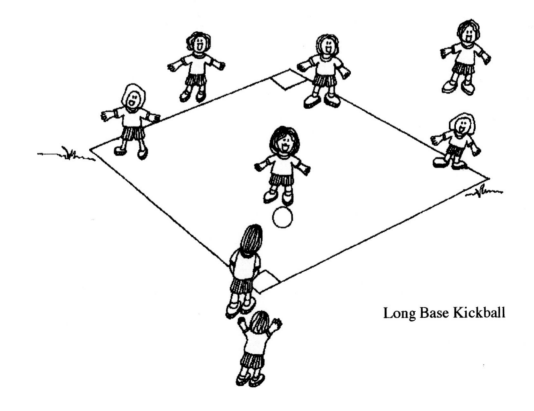

Long Base Kickball

KING SQUARE

WHERE TO PLAY: Outdoors on pavement
NUMBER OF PLAYERS: Four at one time
SUGGESTED GRADE LEVELS: 3nd-8th grades
EQUIPMENT: One playground ball or soccer ball; chalk, if necessary, to mark lines

HOW TO PLAY: Mark off a court that is very much like Four Square, but much larger (16' by 16' up to 40' by 40'). Four Square rules and rotation apply, but the way a player chooses to make contact with the ball differs. Because of the larger court size, a player can (1) catch and punt a ball; (2) catch and throw; (3) use "heading" (as in soccer); (4) use the normal tap used in Four Square. Scoring is the same as in Four Square except players are not penalized for catching a ball hit into their square.

Physical educators might be interested in using this game to develop punting skills by requiring only catching and punting.

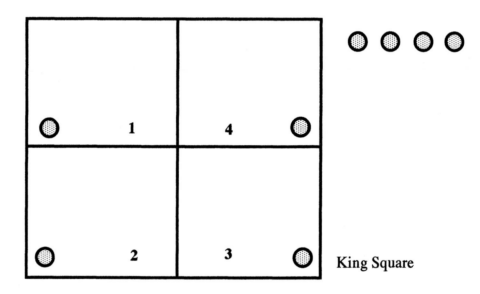

King Square

MAYPOLE

WHERE TO PLAY: Outdoors
NUMBER OF PLAYERS: Any number
GRADE LEVELS: K-4 grades
EQUIPMENT: A long pole or post; paper streamers or ribbons; colored tissue paper; tape

HOW TO PLAY: The Maypole still signifies the coming of spring and is often the centerpiece of May Day celebrations around the world.

To make a Maypole, take an old broom, pole or post, and hang long pieces of ribbon or streamers from the top. The students can tie flowers made from colored tissue paper onto the streamers to beautify the setting.The most popular Maypole activity is to march and dance around the pole. One student holds the pole upright while the other students hold the ends of the streamers and walk around the pole. Maypole music is often included on many folk dance CD's and tapes.

Another Maypole activity is to have the students count off in Ones and Twos. The Ones pass the Twos on the outside, holding the streamers high overhead. The Twos, moving in the opposite direction, pass their streamers over those of the Ones. The Ones and Twos keep alternating until the streamers are woven around the Maypole. When finished, they can unwind them and start over again.

Maypole

TETHERBALL

WHERE TO PLAY: Outdoors
NUMBER OF PLAYERS: 2-6
GRADE LEVELS: 2nd-8th grades
EQUIPMENT: Tetherball and pole
HOW TO PLAY: Tetherball is a mainstay of school playgrounds and one of the more popular

(continued on next page)

Tetherball (cont.)

recess games. Children love the simplicity of the rules and the speed of the ball. This game can be played between two individuals or between two teams, each with 2-3 players.

A typical tetherball court is a circle that is 5 feet in diameter, with the pole in the middle. A line divides the circle into two halves. Players and/or teams must stay on their own half at all times.

The player/team assigned to start first with the ball may bat the ball with their hand either to the right or left. The opposing player/team attempts to bat the ball back in the opposite direction. The two players/teams continue batting the ball back and forth, trying to wrap the ball completely around the pole. This results in a point and the other player/team would get the ball to serve next. Snagging the rope as a means of stopping the rope is prohibited and would result in a free serve for the opponent.

The first player/team to reach 10 points would win the game.

Tetherball

TWO SQUARE

WHERE TO PLAY: On any paved surface
NUMBER PLAYERS: 2 or more
GRADE LEVELS: 1st-8th grades
EQUIPMENT: One playground ball and chalk, if necessary

HOW TO PLAY: The playing area includes two adjoining squares, about four feet on each side. Players stand outside their squares to await the serve. However, once the ball is served players can move inside the square at any time to hit the ball.

Played much like table tennis, one bounce is allowed on each side. Hands instead of paddles are used to hit the ball back and forth instead of paddles. Play continues until one of the two players makes an error, such as hitting it out of bounds or failing to return the ball. If the player who received the serve makes an error, the player who served gains a point. If the player who served makes an error, the ball then is awarded other player to serve. Points can only be earned by the server.

A server continues to serve as long as he is scoring points. The first player to reach 21 points is the winner, provided that he has a 2 point advantage. If not, play continues until one player has won by at least 2 points.

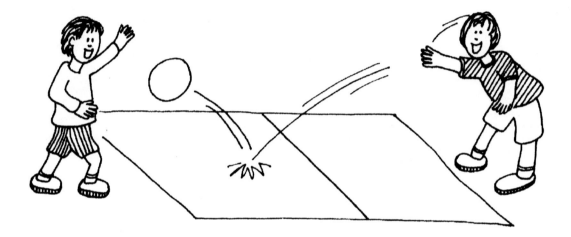

Two Square

WALL BALL

WHERE TO PLAY: Outside
NUMBER OF PLAYERS: 2-6
GRADE LEVELS: 2nd-8th grades
EQUIPMENT: One tennis ball and a wall

HOW TO PLAY: This is a throwing and catching game between two players with the playing area being a wall with a concrete or hard surface. One player begins by throwing the ball, against the

(continued on next page)

Wall Ball (cont.)

 wall with a bounce on the ground first. The opposing player, in turn, must catch the ball before it bounces three times. If not, he is out and the next player in line steps forward to play. If he does catch it, the two players continue throwing and catching in this manner until one player wins. A player gets one point each time he successfully eliminates an opponent.

   A thrower is automatically out when the catcher catches the ball on the fly.

Wall Ball

CHAPTER TWO

SPORTS & SPORT LEAD-UP GAMES

Sports and sport lead-up games bring a unique learning experience to the playground. Participating in sport activities help children develop and refine their physical skills, enhances their fitness level, and provides for significant social growth. This chapter introduces the instructional leader to a wealth of activities to help children learn a variety of team and lifetime sport skills. These games can also launch a lifetime of recreational enjoyment for your students.

BADMINTON

WHERE TO PLAY: Outdoors, or indoors on a court
NUMBER OF PLAYERS: 2-4 on a team
GRADE LEVELS: 3rd-8th grade
EQUIPMENT: A net; one birdie; rackets for each participant

HOW TO PLAY: A regulation court is 45' by 20' for doubles play, and slightly smaller for singles. A service line is marked about 3'- 4' behind the net on both sides of the court.

When playing singles, the server stands behind the service line and hits the birdie underhanded over the net to the opponent's court. The receiver attempts to return the birdie over the net. Both players volley back and forth until the birdie lands on the ground or goes out of bounds. Violations include making more than one hit in succession and touching the net.

The scoring is much like volleyball in that only the serving player scores points. If the serving player makes an error, the opposing player then gets the chance to serve. Play continues until one player scores 21 points and has a two point advantage.

When playing doubles, play progresses much the same way as in single except for the serve. When the first player on a team loses the serve, it goes to his partner to serve next before going over to the opposing team.

Badminton

NO NET BADMINTON

Basically, this game is regular badminton with one exception--there are no nets. This game is particularly helpful in a playground situation where no badminton nets are available. Mark off a court size that is close to regulation badminton dimensions.

Since there is no net, slams are not allowed. The birdie must always be hit with an upward projectory. Otherwise, regular badminton rules apply for both singles and doubles play.

No Net Badminton

BASKETBALL GAMES

WHERE TO PLAY: Regulation basketball requires 2 goals; most of the lead-up games require only one. Basketball playing areas can be found in most playgrounds, gyms, and parks around the world.

NUMBER OF PLAYERS: Regulation basketball rules call for 5 vs. 5 at one time. However, the game can be played with fewer numbers. Most of the basketball lead-up games require at least two players.

GRADE LEVELS: 3rd grade on up.

EQUIPMENT: A basketball and goals.

(continued on next page)

REGULATION BASKETBALL

HOW TO PLAY: Normally, there are five players on each team: one center, two forwards and two guards. To start the game, the official tosses up the ball between two opponents at the center circle. The two jumpers attempt to tap the ball to one of their teammates (who are standing outside the circle). Each team will then try to score by dribbling/passing the ball toward the opponent's goal, and shooting successfully at their basket. After each successful score, the ball is put back into play at the end of the court by the nonscoring team.

A score from the field area is worth two points. A successful free throw shot is worth one point.

A personal foul occurs when a player holds, trips, pushes, charges, blocks, or engages in rough play. If the foul occurs while a player is shooting, the shooter is award two shots from the free throw line. If the shooter made the shot, but was still fouled, he gets one shot from the free throw line. Five personal fouls disqualifies a player from any further participation.

A technical foul occurs when a player acts in an unsportsmanlike manner. The opposing team is awarded two free shots and possession of the ball afterward.

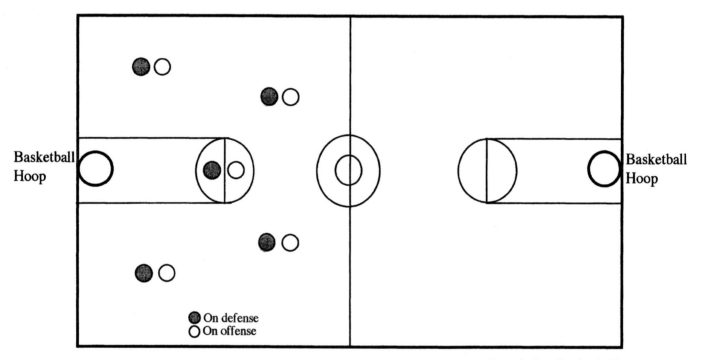

Basketball Hoop

Basketball Hoop

● On defense
○ On offense

Regulation Basketball

All violations result in the opposing team throwing the ball in from the nearest out-of- bounds spot. Violations are:

1) traveling--taking more than one step while in possession of the ball; 2) double Dribbling-- dribbling with two hands or dribbling a second time after having stopped the first dribbling series.

3) kicking the ball; 4) three seconds in the key – offensive player standing inside the key area for three seconds. 5) Taking more than –10 seconds for the offensive team to cross the mid-court line. 6) out-of-bounds ball stepping on the out-of-bounds line while in possession of the ball, or passing or knocking the ball out of bounds.

A game is normally played in quarters or two halves, the length of which can be decided by the two teams. The team with the highest score wins.

HALF-COURT BASKETBALL

   This is a favorite playground and home driveway basketball game and a popular choice for those situations in which only one goal is available for a game. Additionally, it can allow for two games to be played on one regulation court at the same time resulting in more players being actively involved.

   Played like regulation basketball, the out-of-bounds lines include the standard lines plus the center line. Teams can play three-on-three, four-on-four or five-on-five.

   The game begins with a jump ball at the free throw line. After that, regular rules apply except: (1) when the offensive team scores, the opposing team will throw the ball in from out of bounds at the center line; (2) if the defensive team gets possession of the ball, they must dribble or pass it past the free throw line before scoring.

   Scoring is the same as in regulation basketball.

Half-Court Basketball

HORSE

Horse is probably the playground's most frequently played basketball shooting game. Played with one goal, two players decide between themselves who will shoot first.

The game begins with the first shooter taking a shot from anywhere on the court. If the ball goes in, the second shooter must make it from that same spot. If the second shooter misses, the letter "H" is assigned. If he makes it, no letter is given.

Horse

When the first shooter misses a shot, the second shooter then gets the chance to make a shot which must be duplicated. As the players make and miss baskets, the opportunity of the first shot will pass quite frequently between the two players. The letters H-O-R-S-E are assigned to players that miss shots that must be duplicated.

The first player that has H-O-R-S-E spelled against him loses.

AROUND THE WORLD

This shooting game is played with one goal. The objective is to make baskets from eight spots in a semicircular pattern around the goal, and then do the same going in the opposite direction.

The player chosen to shoot first shoots from spot #1 (at the base of the key). If the shot is good, he moves up to the next spot. If he misses, the second player then gets a turn at shooting from spot #1. Play continues with each player shooting from the spot they last missed from.

The first player that first successfully makes all the shots (spots 1-8 and back again) wins the game.

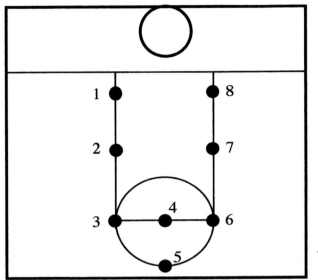

Around The World

TWENTY-ONE

Twenty-One combines foul shooting with one-on-one half-court basketball. The game begins one player shooting from the foul line and the other player acting as a rebounder underneath the goal. If the shooter makes the first basket, he earns two points; thereafter, each basket is worth one point. He continues shooting until he misses. Upon a miss the rebounder may attempt to get possession of the ball and shoot. If the ball goes in, he earns a point, and the players exchange positions.

The first player to score 21 points wins the game. However, the winner must score 21 exactly. If a player goes over 21, he loses. Therefore, a player with 20 points should deliberately miss a shot from the foul line, hoping to rebound and make one point.

Twenty-One

NO RULES BASKETBALL

This is a fun game for the younger and/or less skilled child. It's basketball with as few rules possible!

Assign one team to start with the ball from their backcourt area. The players are allowed to dribble, walk or run with the ball, and can take as long as they want to move the ball down the court. Since no traveling or double dribble violations exist in this game, players have freedom in how they choose to move with the ball.

Players on defense are not allowed to take a ball from an offensive player, nor are they allowed to touch or foul a player. Defensive players can only gain possession of the ball off a rebound, a dropped ball by an offensive player, or an interception of a pass.

A successful shot counts as two points. The team at the end with the highest point total wins.

KNOCK OUT

This is another fun shooting game that requires only one goal. The objective is to "knock out" of the game another player by making a basket ahead of him. An ideal number of participants is three or four players. They then decide a shooting order and stand in a file at the foul line.

The first player shoots from the foul line. If the shot is good, he goes to the back of the line and remains in the game. If he misses, he gets his rebound and continues shooting until either he makes it or the second player has made a basket. If the second player makes a basket before the first player, the first player is "knocked out" and must exit the game. The remaining players continue playing with "knock outs" occurring every time a player makes a basket before the player ahead of him.

The winner is the last player remaining.

Knock Out

40

TRIPLE PLAY

This game is played very much like half-court basketball except three players are playing at the same time, each being his own team. It's basically one-on-one-on-one.

The game begins with one player on offense first with the ball. The other two players are on defense until one of them steals the ball or gets a rebound off a missed shot. This player would then become the new offensive player. If an offensive player makes a shot, he continues being the offensive player. If the defensive players force the offensive player to stop dribbling, then the offensive player is forced to shoot from that spot and must do so within three seconds.

A player gets two points for each shot made. At the end, the player with the highest point total wins.

Triple Play

GOTCHA!

This is a great game that develops dribbling skills and involves no goals. All players need a basketball. On a starting signal, the players are to dribble randomly within a marked playing area, while at the same time trying to knock away other players' basketballs with their free hand. Players yell out "Gotcha" when they knock away another player's basketball and receive one point for doing so. If a player has his ball knocked away, he is to quickly retrieve it and rejoin the game. Players have to dribble continuously throughout the playing of the game.

One point is given for each basketball that a player knocks away. The player with the highest point total wins.

(continued on next page)

Gotcha!

<u>BULL IN THE RING</u>

   This passing and catching game of keep-away is a recess favorite. Form groups of 6-8 players with each group standing in a circle formation. Assign one player to stand in the middle and be the "Bull."

   On a starting signal, the players pass a basketball back and forth among themselves while, at the same time, the Bull attempts to touch or intercept it. If a ball is touched by the Bull, then the player who last touched it switches places and becomes the next Bull. Players can not throw a pass to the player to either side of them, nor can they throw it to the player who threw it to them.

   The player who has been the Bull the least often is declared the game winner.

Bull in the Ring

BASKETBALL PIRATES

This is a challenging and fun activity for developing dribbling skills. With the exception of several players (the Pirates), start by having the players stand with a basketball throughout the playing area. On a signal, the players without a basketball (the Pirates) chase the dribblers and attempt to steal their basketballs. Once a dribbler loses his ball to a Pirate, he becomes the next Pirate. A pirate can not steal a basketball from the player who stole it from him. Dribblers have to dribble continuously throughout the game. The game winners are the ones at the end who have been Pirates the least often.

Basketball Pirates

TEAM THREE-ON-THREE

This game is played very much like Half-Court Basketball (see description) with the exception that a third team rotates into the game after each score. Two teams start play on the court with a third team standing on a sideline. Once a team has been scored against, they switch places with the team that has been waiting on the sideline. Other than this, the rules for Half-Court Basketball apply. The team with the highest score at the end of a predetermined time period wins.

CRICKET BALL

WHERE TO PLAY: Outside
NUMBER OF PLAYERS: Four players to a game; multiple games can be played simultaneously.
SUGGESTED GRADE LEVELS: 2nd-8th grades
EQUIPMENT: One base; one cone; one bat; and one softball

HOW TO PLAY: Set a cone and base in a straight line about 30-40 feet apart. Assign four players to each game; a pitcher, batter, catcher, and fielder.

The pitcher begins by throwing the ball toward the cone, which the batter is standing in front of and off to the side. If the pitcher hits the cone, it counts as a strike. If the batter hits the ball, he runs to the base and back (without stopping) before the catcher is thrown the ball. If successful, the batter scores a run for himself. If unsuccessful, the batter is out. Unlike softball, tagging and catching fly hits do not count as outs.

After each out or run, players are to rotate positions. The batter becomes the next fielder; the fielder moves up to pitcher; the pitcher goes to catcher; and the catcher becomes the new batter.

Cricket Ball

FOOTBALL GAMES

WHERE TO PLAY: Outside
NUMBER OF PLAYERS: 4 or more
GRADE LEVELS: 3rd-8th grades
EQUIPMENT: A football

TOUCH FOOTBALL

HOW TO PLAY: Touch Football is a modified version of regulation and flag football. In most school playground situations, a regulation size football field is too long. A field length of about 40 yards would be sufficient for elementary aged students. Although team sizes can range between 2-11 players, an ideal number is 4-6 players.

In this game, a player is "tackled," and the ball is downed when the ballcarrier is tagged with both hands simultaneously by a defensive player. To guard against rough play, a 15 yard penalty can be assessed against the defensive team if they unnecessarily slap, shove, or push a ballcarrier when attempting a tackle.

The game starts with a kick-off from midfield. Someone on the receiving team should attempt to catch the ball and run it toward the opposing team's goal line. When " tackled," the ball is dead and is placed at that spot. (continued next page)

Touch Football

Touch Football (cont.)

To simplify the game for recess and informal play, no automatic first downs are awarded to a team for gaining 10 yards (as in regulation football). The offensive team has only four tries or "downs" to move the ball to the opponents' goal line and score.

When the quarterback says "Hike," the offensive players can go into motion. All forward passes must be thrown from behind the line of scrimmage and all offensive players are eligible to receive a pass. An incomplete pass results in the ball reverting back to the previous line of scrimmage (or the spot where the ball became "dead").

Defensive players try to prevent the pass from being completed by closely guarding each offensive player. A defensive player can knock the ball away from a receiver's hands, as long as he doesn't touch the player. A pass interference penalty will result in a completed pass at the spot of the foul. A pass may also be intercepted by any defensive player.

If the offensive team manages to cross the opponents' goal line with the ball on one of their four downs, a touchdown is scored worth six points. If the offensive team fails to score on their four tries, the ball is awarded to the other team at that spot. They will then be awarded four downs to score going the opposite direction.

On a fourth down, an offensive team has the option of running a regular play or punting. A team will often punt when they aren't close to their opponents' goal line and feel that they need to kick the ball and put the other team as far from their goal line as possible.

After each touchdown, the scoring team kicks off the other team. At the conclusion of the game, the team with the most points wins.

HOME RUN FOOTBALL

This is a fun combination of football and softball. A softball field is needed with all players given a number. The first player stands at home base with the football. The rest of the players need to scatter throughout the infield and outfield.

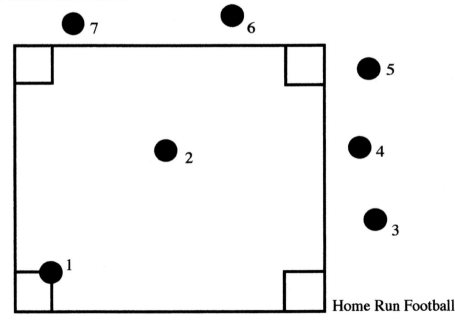

Home Run Football

The game begins with the first player passing, punting or kicking the football out into the field. He then runs the bases as quickly as possible, just as in softball. The players in the field retrieve the football and try to either throw, kick or run it in to home base. At that time, the runner stops.

Each runner is awarded one point for each base touched before the ball reached home base. After play has stopped, the runner then goes out into the field and the player with the next number then gets a chance to throw, punt or kick and then run the bases.

Each player is to keep track of their score. The player with the highest score wins.

CAPTURE THE FOOTBALLS

This game is a variation of Capture the Flags. A rectangular size playing area is needed, along with four footballs, flags for each player, two long ropes, and two large hula hoops. Cones can be used for boundary lines if none exist. The two long ropes are to be used for prison markings. The two footballs are put in each team's hula hoop (see illustration below). Divide the players into two equal teams and have each team start by standing on their "home" turf.

The game begins with some of the players from each team crossing the center line, attempting to capture the footballs while others stay back and defend. The objective is for one team to capture their opponents' two footballs while, at the same time keeping its own two footballs from being stolen. Once a team has all four footballs inside its hula hoop, the game is either finished or a score has occurred.

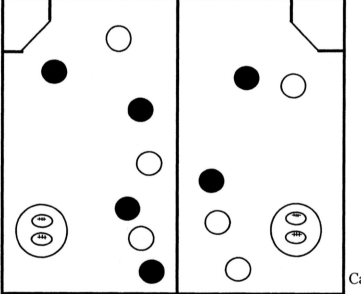
Capture the Footballs

Players attempting to steal a football may do so by running with it back toward their home side, or passing it to a teammate in their home territory. A ball that is dropped must be returned to the hula hoop. Additionally, any player who has his flag pulled while running with a football must put it back inside the hula hoop.

All players who have one of their flags pulled while in their opponent's territory must go to their prison. Prisoners can be freed by having a teammate successfully make it into the prison and walk them back to their home side.

ONE CHANCE FOOTBALL

Although this game is played very much like Touch Football, it differs in that every play is a "fourth" down with each team trying to score a touchdown on that one play. Another difference is that players receiving a pass from the quarterback have the same privileges and can pass at any time, from any spot, and in any direction. There can be an unlimited number of passes on any play, either from behind the line of scrimmage or forward. A touchdown is scored if a player crosses the goal line with the ball.

A play is over when any of the following has occurred: an incomplete pass, an interception, a player with the ball is "tackled" (that is, touched with two hands), a fumble, or a player with the ball runs out of bounds.

After each play, the opposing team gets the football at midfield for their one chance to score. No kicking or punting is allowed.

A team receives six points for each touchdown scored. The team with the highest score at the end wins.

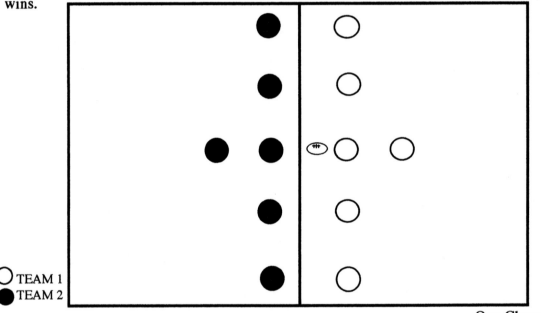

One Chance Football

END ZONE

This is a fantastic game for development of throwing and catching skills. Using cones, mark off a field as shown below. Divide the players into two equal teams with half of each team standing in a designated end zone.

The objective is to throw a football into the end zone and have it caught by a teammate for a score. Players can run up to the center line (but cannot cross it) to throw the football past opposing players to an awaiting teammate. Likewise, defensive players can run up to the center line or end zone line to block or knock down a pass, but cannot cross either line. Footballs that go into the end zone are thrown back to their teammates. Only catches made by end zone players count as points. Have teammates switch positions halfway through the contest. Add additional footballs throughout the playing of the game.

A team receives one point for each catch made by an end zone player. The team at the end with the highest point total wins.

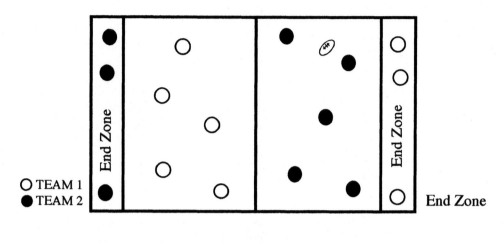

FAKE 'EM OUT

Set up a playing area that is about 30 by 50 feet in size, with a marked off "No-Man's Territory" in the middle (see illustration). Divide players into two teams with each team having half of its members on each side of the No-Man's Territory. Both teams start with a one football (more can be added later in the game).

The objective is to complete a pass to a teammate on the other side of the No-Man's Territory. Emphasize that the receivers need to run and fake out the defenders in order to get themselves open for a pass. No player can cross into the No-Man's Territory, nor is any rough play, tackling, blocking, or interference allowed.

A team earns one point for each completed pass. Designate certain players to help keep score as they're playing.

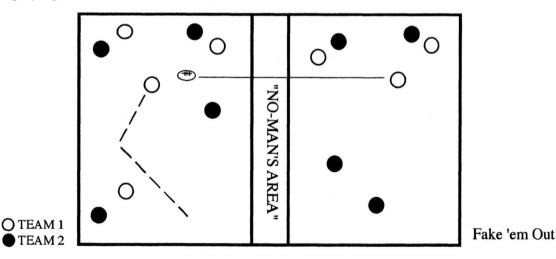

Fake 'em Out

FIVE CATCHES

Form two teams with five players each. Multiple games can be played simultaneously if space allows. Pinnies should be worn to distinguish the two teams. A marked off playing area that is about 30 by 50 feet is ideal.

The objective is for a team to make five consecutive passes to five different players without dropping the ball or having it intercepted. To begin, have the players scatter throughout the playing area. Each player is assigned to guard one player on the opposing team. The player with the ball can not take more than three steps when attempting to throw to a teammate, nor can he hold the ball for more than five seconds. Either of these violations results in the opposing team gaining possession of the ball.

A team to make five successful catches scores one point. The team with the highest point total at the end of play wins the game.

Five Catches

FRISBEE GOLF

WHERE TO PLAY: Outside
NUMBER OF PLAYERS: 2-5 players to each course
GRADE LEVELS: 3rd-8th grades
EQUIPMENT: One frisbee for each player; nine hula hoops; nine numbered cones

HOW TO PLAY: Set up the golf course by placing hula hoops about 20'- 40' apart in a scattered formation. Put a numbered cone (1-9) in the middle of each hula hoop. Assign 2-5 players to each course.

To begin, a player throws a frisbee toward the first hole (the hula hoop), hoping to land it inside the hula hoop. In order, the other players do the same. Continue until all the players have "holed out." The player with the lowest score (that is, the fewest throws attempted for the frisbee to finally land inside the hula hoop) is allowed to throw first for the next hole.

The player completing the course in the fewest number of "strokes" is the winner.

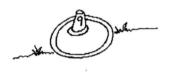

Frisbee Golf

MINI-TEAM HANDBALL

WHERE TO PLAY: Can be played outside or in a gym; a 30' by 60' playing area will work fine with most elementary grades.

NUMBER OF PLAYERS: Two teams of 4-6 players each

GRADE LEVELS: 4th-8th grades

EQUIPMENT: Six cone markers; pinnies; six beanbags

HOW TO PLAY: This is a lead-up game that is very successful for developing skills and strategies related to the international game of Team Handball.

First, it is helpful for players to wear pinnies so that teams can be distinguished from each other. Each team needs to have a goalie. Behind each goal needs to be three cones with a beanbag resting on the top of each one. The objective is to score by throwing a ball past the goalie and knocking one of the beanbags off a cone.

(continued on next page)

Mini-Team Handball (cont.)

The game begins with a jump ball in the middle of the playing area. Players can only pass to a team mate or throw at the goal. No running or steps are allowed once a player has possession of the ball. Also, a player only has up to 5 seconds to pass or shoot. Any of these violations will result in the other team taking possession of the ball at that spot.

Defensive players are to guard an offensive player much as in basketball. Touching an offensive player is not allowed, nor can a defensive player knock the ball out of an opponent's hands.

After each score, the team that was scored against takes possession of the ball at midfield and the game continues. One point is scored for each goal.

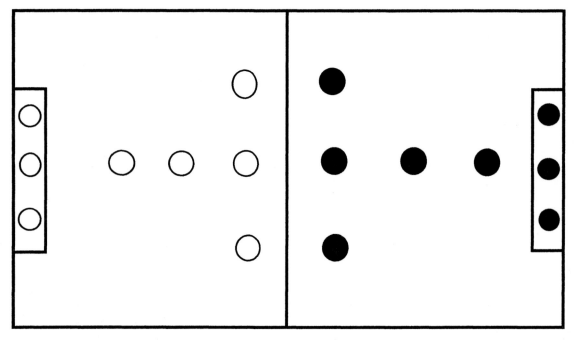

Mini-Team Handball

OUTSIDE FIELD BILLIARDS

WHERE TO PLAY: Outside; a 25' by 35' billiard shaped playing area would be ideal.
NUMBER OF PLAYERS: Two teams of two players each; set up multiple playing areas for larger groups.
GRADE LEVELS: 3rd-8th grades

EQUIPMENT: Ten soccer balls; one playground ball; twelve cones

HOW TO PLAY: This is a great activity for practicing kicking skills and introducing the elements of playing billards. The additional physical exercise that comes from playing outside adds the appeal of this game.

First, set up a 25' by 35' playing area (see illustration), with two cones placed about 2' apart at each of the six billiard "pockets." The ten soccer balls need to be placed in a tight, triangular shaped formation at one end of the field, with the cue ball (playground ball) at the other end.

Players take turns kicking the cue ball (playground ball) at the billiard balls (soccer balls). The objective is to knock a soccer ball into a "pocket" (through the cones). Just as in regulation billiards, a player continues to "shoot" as long as he makes his shots.

The player with the highest number of balls hit through the pockets wins.

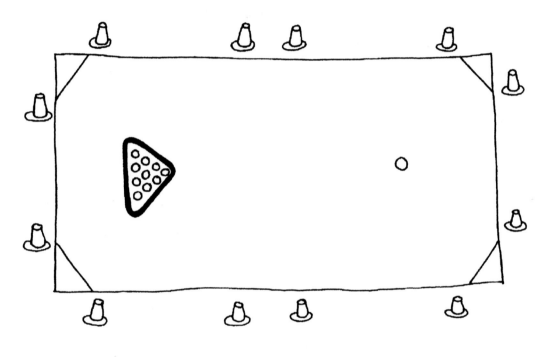

Outside Field Billiards

SCOOP LACROSSE

WHERE TO PLAY: Outside on a soccer field

NUMBER OF PLAYERS: Two teams of 6-11 players each is ideal

SUGGESTED GRADE LEVELS: 4th-8th grades

EQUIPMENT: One plastic scoop or milk carton box (a one gallon plastic milk jug with the bottom half cut off) for each player; one whiffle or tennis ball; pinnies

(Continued on next page)

Scoop Lacrosse(cont.)

HOW TO PLAY: This is a wonderful adapted version of the game of lacrosse using plastic scoops or milk jugs instead of lacrosse sticks.

One team starts with possession of the ball at midfield. The player with the ball begins the game by throwing to a teammate. Offensive players attempt to move the ball down the field toward their goal by throwing, catching, and running with the ball. The ball can only be played with the scoop; that is, no hands can be used to scoop a ball up or to catch it. Players are not allowed to throw the ball to themselves.

Defensive players are to guard offensive players, much as in basketball. Defenders should be warned not to hit or grab the ball out of an opponent's scoop. This illegal contact results in a penalty throw (much as a penalty kick in soccer).

Goalies are to stay inside a marked goalie area. No other players are allowed inside this area. The goalie can block a scoring attempt by using his legs or by catching the ball. A ball that is blocked may be picked up by the goalie, put into his scoop and thrown back into the field of play. If a score is made, the goalie puts the ball back into play and the game continues. One point is awarded to a team each time the ball is thrown into the goal.

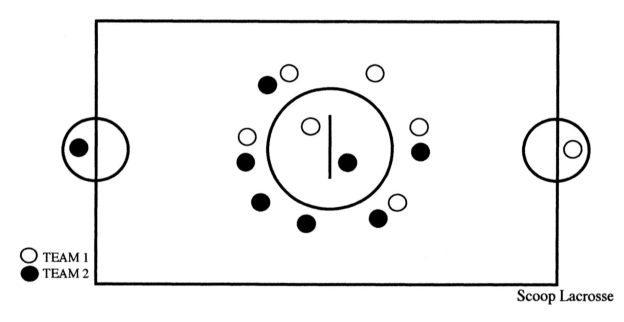

○ TEAM 1
● TEAM 2

Scoop Lacrosse

SOCCER

WHERE TO PLAY: Soccer field
NUMBER OF PLAYERS: 11 on a team for regulation soccer; less for lead-up games
GRADE LEVELS: K-8 grades
EQUIPMENT: One soccer ball for regulation play; more for some of the lead-up games.

REGULATION SOCCER

HOW TO PLAY: Soccer is unique among playground sport games in that children as young as five years of age can successfully participate, understand, and enjoy this relatively simple game. It's basically a running and kicking game in which the ball is normally controlled by the foot, body, or head. The ball may not be touched with the hands or arms.

The game is played by two teams of 11 players each. The Goalie (or goalkeeper) prevents the ball from going into the goal; two Fullbacks play out in front of the goalie and play defense; three Halfbacks move with ball and play both defense and offense; and the five Forwards main responsibility is to advance the ball and score.

At the start of the game, the selection of a team to kick-off first is made along with goal selection. The center forward of the offensive team kicks the ball from the center circle to a teammate. The ball must travel forward at least one yard. On the kickoff, the defensive team must be 10 yards from the kicker, and both teams need to be onside. After the kickoff, players on both teams may cross the center line and play the ball. The object of the game is to move the ball down the field and into the opponent's goal for a score. The ball is moved by dribbling or passing to another teammate. A defending player may intercept the ball and advance the ball the opposite direction.

A team that successfully scores a goal is awarded one point. The team scored against then gets to kickoff.

During the game, if the ball goes out-of-bounds on the sideline, the ball is put into play with a throw-in from the spot where it crossed the line. A throw-in is delivered with two hands on the ball, over the top of the head, with both feet in contact with the ground.

If the ball goes out of bounds past the end line by the offensive team, a goal kick is awarded with the goalie on the defensive team kicking the ball back into play. If the defensive team causes the ball to cross past its own goal line, a corner kick is awarded to the offensive team.

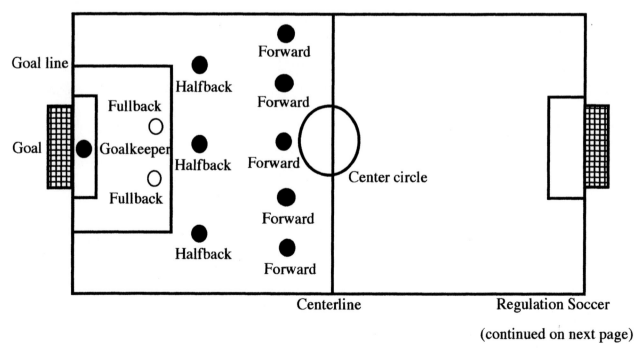

Regulation Soccer

(continued on next page)

Regulation Soccer (cont.)

Other than the goalie, it is a foul for any player to touch the ball with their hands or arms. A free kick is awarded to the opponents at that spot. Unnecessary roughness, such as pushing, charging, tripping, holding or striking an opponent also results in a free kick. Another violation resulting in a free kick is called for being offsides. This occurs any time an attacking player, while in his opponent's half of the field, does not have at least two opponents in front of him at the time the ball was advanced forward.

MODIFIED SOCCER

This game is played very much like regulation soccer but without the required number of players on the field at one time. Each team has one goalie, three forwards, two halfbacks and one fullback. This is an ideal number of participates for the many elementary schools and parks that now have "mini" soccer fields (that is, smaller soccer field dimensions).

Regulation soccer rules and scoring, as explained above, apply.

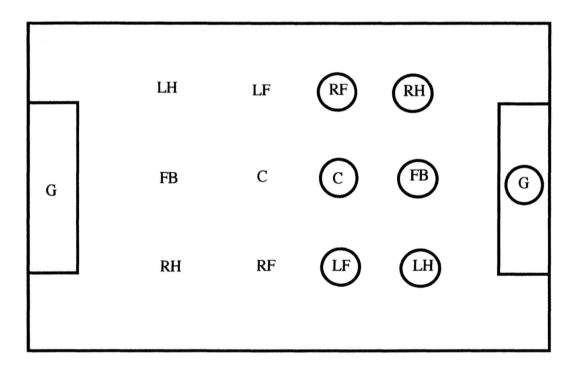

MASS SOCCER

This is a simple version of soccer with few rules, making it a great activity for younger and/or less skilled students. Divide a group into two equal teams with each team lined up on an end line. Place a soccer ball in the middle of the playing area. On a starting signal, both teams run forward from their end lines and attempt to gain possession of the soccer ball. The team with possession wants to kick the ball over the opponent's end line, below shoulder level, for a score.

There are no set positions, and players are free to roam the playing area. No player is allowed to use hands (there are no goalies). As in regulation soccer, a goal counts as one point.

Mass Soccer

3-ON-3 SOCCER

This game is played much like regulation soccer except there are only three players on a team and the field is smaller (about 40' by 60' is ideal). Cones can used for goal markers. One player for each team should start in the goalie position with the other two players at midfield.

The game begins with one team kicking off. Teams try to score by kicking the ball through the opponent's cones. A kickoff follows each score, with players rotating positions. Rotating allows equal opportunities to play both goalie and forward.

Regulation soccer rules apply to scoring, hand violations, out of bounds, and rough play.

3-On-3 Soccer

CRAB SOCCER

Because the participants are required to be in a crab position, this game is best played in the gymnasium. Two foam soccer balls are placed in the middle of the court, with each team on their own side before starting play. On a starting signal, both teams move forward and attempt to move the balls over their opponent's end line (while in a crab position). Hands can not be used to hit the ball. After a score, simply place the ball back in the middle for non-stop action (the other ball remains in play). One point is scored for each ball that crosses the opponent's end line.

Crab Soccer

SOCCER BULL

This soccer version of "keep-a-way" is played with a group of 5-10 players standing in a circle with one player in the middle (the "Bull").

Soccer Bull

On a starting signal, the circle players begin passing a soccer ball from one player to another, trying to keep it away from the "Bull" who is attempting to touch or intercept the ball with his feet or body. If the "Bull" is successful, he switches places with the player who last touched the ball. If a ball goes outside the circle, the player responsible becomes the next "Bull." The player, at the end, who has been the Bull the least often is the winner.

SOCCER CROQUET

This terrific game is played much like regular croquet except players kick soccer balls instead of hitting balls with a mallet through wire wickets. The objective is to be the first player to go to the halfway point, turn around, and return home. As in regular croquet, the ball needs to be hit (or in this case, kicked) through the cones going forward before advancing to the next "wicket." Also, everyone has the right to knock another player's ball with their own. Players stay in the same kicking order throughout the game. The first player to complete the course is the winner.

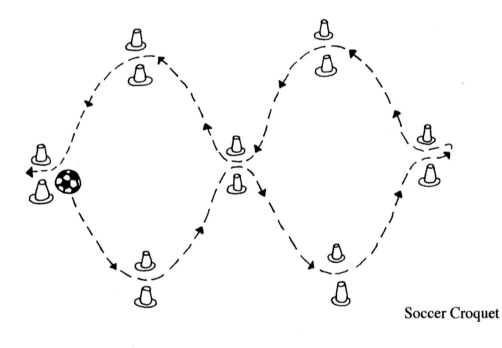

Soccer Croquet

SOCCER GOLF

Basically, this game is golf with kicking instead of swinging. First, set up a golf course by placing hula hoops about 30'- 60' apart in a scattered formation. Put a numbered cone marker (1-9) in the middle of each hula hoop. An ideal number of players on one course is 3-5; set up multiple courses for larger groups.

To begin, a player kicks a soccer ball toward the first hole (the hula hoop), trying to have it land

(continued on next page)

Soccer Golf (cont.)

inside the hoop. In order, the rest of the players do the same. Continue until all the players have "holed out." The player with the lowest score (that is, the fewest shots attempted to get the ball into the hula hoop) kicks first for the next hole. At the end, the player with the lowest overall score wins.

Soccer Golf

FOUR BALL SHOOTOUT

This is regulation soccer but with four balls being used instead of one. On a starting signal, players attempt to gain possession of the four balls and kick them into the opposing team's goal for a score. After the start, players are free to roam the playing area. When a goal has been scored, the player that made the goal (not the goalie) returns the ball to the center area to kick again. This is a continual action game with all soccer balls played simultaneously. Teams are to keep track of their running score.

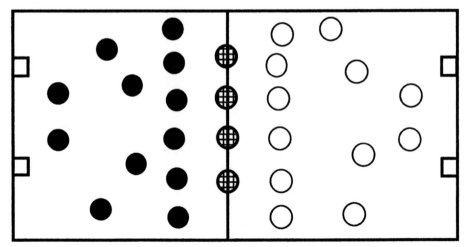

Four Ball Shootout

DRIBBLE FREEZE TAG

This is a terrific mixture of tag and soccer. Use a gymnasium or an outside playing area that is about 20 x 30 yards in size. With the exception of three players (who are the "Its" and do not have a ball), all players need to stand scattered around the playing area with a foot on a soccer ball.

On a starting signal, the players begin dribbling randomly within the playing area. At the same time, the Its attempt to tag the dribblers. A dribbler that is tagged has to stop and sit on their ball. He is "frozen" until a free dribbler gets close enough to touch them on the shoulder, thereby "unfreezing" him. Players who end up being tagged the least often are the winners.

Dribble Freeze Tag

CIRCLE SOCCER

Form two teams of 6-8 players and have each team make a semicircle. Players should stand a couple of feet apart.

(continued on next page)

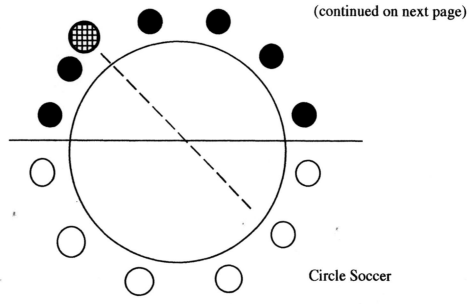

Circle Soccer

Circle Soccer (cont.)

On a starting signal, the players attempt to kick the ball below shoulder level past the other team. Players should try to trap a ball before kicking. No hands can used at anytime during the game.

If the ball comes to a stop inside the circle, have a player closest to the ball return it back to his spot and kick again. Consider adding a second ball halfway through the game.

One point is awarded to a team for each kick that goes past the opponents (below shoulder level).

PIN SOCCER

This fun activity develops kicking accuracy and trapping. Form two teams of 5-10 players with the teams facing each other on opposite lines that are 10-15 yards apart. A row of bowling pins stands in the middle of the two lines. Each team starts with 3-5 soccer balls.

On a starting signal, the players attempt to kick and knock down as many bowling pins as possible from behind their lines. Players should trap the ball before kicking. When all the pins have been knocked over, stop play and ask which team hit the most pins. A team receives one point for winning each round. Reset the pins and play again.

A designated player, or the game leader, should retrieve and equally distribute any soccer balls that come to a stop in the middle area.

Pin Soccer

62

SOFTBALL

WHERE TO PLAY: An official softball diamond has 60 foot baselines and a 46 foot pitching distance. Most K-8 schools will have a field smaller in size.
NUMBER OF PLAYERS: Two teams of nine players each; a pitcher, catcher, first baseman, second baseman, third baseman, shortstop, right fielder, center fielder, and left fielder.
GRADE LEVELS: 3rd-8th graders
EQUIPMENT: A softball, bases, and bat; gloves for harder softballs

HOW TO PLAY: Assign one team to take fielding positions (see illustration) and the other to bat. The batting team establishes a set batting order. The first batter stands at home base and attempts to hit an underhanded pitched ball in such a way that allows him to get on base without getting out. The objective for a batter is to successfully circle the bases (either on his hit or his teammates' hits) and score a run. Batters are allowed three strikes before being called out. Foul balls count as strikes, but a foul cannot count as third strike.

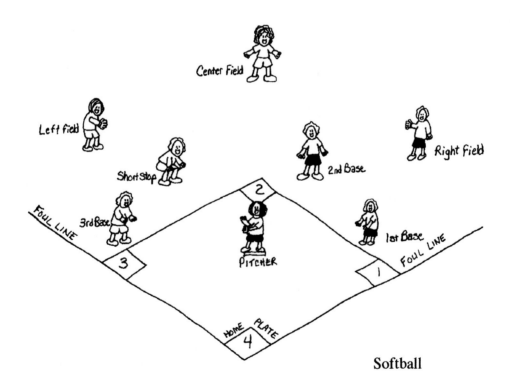

Softball

 Besides striking out a batter, the fielding team can get the batter and any baserunners out by any of the following means:
-- batter is tagged out running to first base;
-- batter hits a foul or fair fly ball that is caught;

(continued on next page)

Softball (cont.)

-- batter bunts the ball foul on a third strike;

-- batter throws the bat outside the batter's circle;

-- a baserunner is tagged when off a base;

-- a baserunner is forced to run to the next base, but the fielding team touches the base first;

-- a baserunner passes another baserunner;

-- a baserunner leaves a base before the ball has left the pitcher's hand (there's no "leading-off").

Each team continues to bat until it has made three outs, at which time the teams switch places. After both teams have batted, an inning is completed. The team that has scored the most runs after a predetermined number of innings is the winner.

THREE TEAM SOFTBALL

This is a great game for those occasions when you want to eliminate the waiting time for batters, and provide the opportunity for students to play multiple positions.

The rules of softball apply with the exception that these three teams are competing against each other at the same time. Each team should have 4-6 players. Team #1 begins at bat. Team #2 assumes the infield positions. Team #3 is stationed in the outfield (see illustration).

When team #1 has committed 3 outs, all the teams rotate. Team #1 moves to the outfield, team #2 becomes the next batters, and team #3 moves up into the infield positions. An inning includes all three teams having a chance to bat.

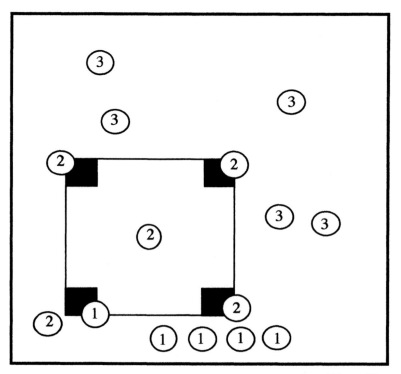

Three Team Softball

MODIFIED SLO-PITCH

This is played exactly like regular softball with the following exceptions: the pitcher must pitch a slow underhanded toss; the batter cannot bunt; no base stealing is allowed; a team continues to bat (regardless of the number of outs) until everyone has batted before switching with the fielding team.

These modified rules allow for greater success with the younger players and prevents one team from being at bat the majority of the time.

NO-OUTS SOFTBALL

This is an exciting variation of softball that your students will enjoy. No-Outs Softball is played with regular softball positions except it works best to have the pitcher be a member of the batting team.

The objective for each batter is to hit the pitched ball out into fair territory and run the bases without stopping until the catcher gains possession of the ball and yells out "freeze." This is the signal for the baserunner to stop running and to stay in that position, even if he is not on a base. When the next batter hits the ball, the baserunner(s) start running again around the bases until the next freeze signal. Each time a baserunner touches home base counts as one point for that team. The baserunners do not stop after circling the bases once, but rather continue to run and score until everyone on their team has batted. There are no outs. Teams switch places after every batter has had a chance to hit and run.

No-Outs Softball

65

NO-TEAM SOFTBALL

It's each player against everyone else! As its name implies, this game has no set teams and each player's objective is to ouster all the others. This game is played with regular softball positions, except players will rotate after each out according to the illustration shown below.

A batter continues to bat and run the bases as long as he is successful. He gets one point for himself each time he circles the bases and touches home base. If the batter/baserunner gets out, he rotates to the right field position. Everyone else rotates one spot as well, with the catcher becoming the next batter.

Players are to keep their own individual score. The player with the highest individual score at the end would be declared the overall winner.

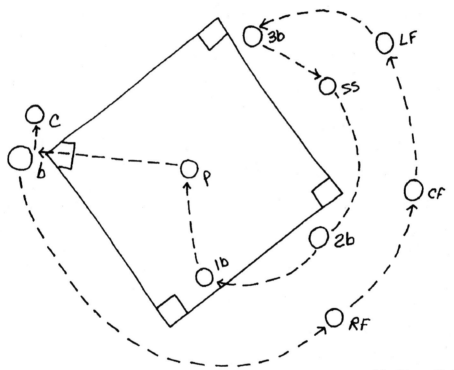

No-Team Softball

THROW SOFTBALL

This game is played very much like regulation softball except that the batter, instead of batting the ball, catches the pitcher's pitch and immediately throws it anywhere in the field. The ball is played by the fielding team as it would in regular softball.

Specific rules for this game also include: (1) The batter is out if he drops a pitched ball that was in the strike zone; (2) A ball thrown by the batter into foul territory is considered an out; (3) There is no base stealing.

Throw Softball

PICKLE

A baserunner is in a "pickle" when he is caught between two bases, with the possibility of getting run down and tagged. This fun activity makes a contest of this common game situation.

First, three players need to be assigned to a group, with two players occupying the two bases and the third standing halfway between the two bases. The objective of the player in the middle is to reach one of the two bases without getting tagged with the ball. The two fielders attempt to tag the runner by throwing the ball back and forth, running toward him so he can be tagged. The baserunner gets one point if he safely reaches a base. After each play, the players rotate so that all have an equal number of chances at running.

Pickle

ONE CHANCE SOFTBALL

Here is a game that will virtually guarantee a lot of individual batting opportunities. This activity is played exactly like regulation softball except the batter is allowed only one chance to hit the pitched ball. Because of this rule, it works best if the pitcher is a member of the batting team.

In addition to regular softball outs, the batter is out if he hits a ball into foul territory. There is also no bunting; if a batter attempts a bunt, he is called out.

Scoring is the same as regulation softball.

ADD 'EM UP

This game is played very much like regulation softball except for the scoring– which can add up in a hurry! Batters receive one point for reaching first base safely, two points for getting to second base, three points for third base and four points for a home run. The batting team should count out loud their team score when a team mate is running the bases and scoring points. Everyone bats before switching.

Add 'Em Up

VOLLEYBALL

WHERE TO PLAY: Indoors on a standard court, or outside

NUMBER OF PLAYERS: Regulation volleyball calls for 6 on a side; however, most elementary games can accommodate up to 9 players.

GRADE LEVELS: 3rd-8th grades

EQUIPMENT: A net and volleyball; adjust the height according to the age and/or skill level of your students.

HOW TO PLAY: Players should take positions on a court as shown in the illustration below. One team is designated to serve first. The server stands behind the boundary line in the right back row and hits the ball (either underhand or overhand) over the net. If the serve fails to go over the net inbounds, the serve goes to the other team. If the serve is successful, the receiving team has up to three hits to return it over the net. The ball is volleyed back and forth over the net until one team fails to return it. If the non-serving team makes the error, the serving team scores a point. The serving team keeps the serve until they make an error.

Only the serving team can score. The first team to 15 points wins, provided they have a two point advantage; otherwise, play continues until one team has a two point advantage.

Important rules that players should know include:

(1) A team gaining the serve must have its players rotate clockwise one position.

(2) The ball can not be caught, held, or carried.

(3) Players can not touch the net; nor can they reach over or cross under the net.

(4) The same player can not touch the ball twice in succession.

(5) Any ball that lands on a boundary line is considered in-bounds.

Volleyball

BEACHBALL VOLLEYBALL

This game is played very much like regulation volleyball, except a beachball is used instead of a regular volleyball. This is a super game for the beginning volleyball player as the bigger ball makes it much easier to react and make contact. A few rule changes, such as the ones below, can be implemented to make the game even more successful and enjoyable for the younger players.

(1) Serves can be "helped" over the net by fellow teammates.

(2) Players are allowed to touch the net during play.

(3) Teams are allowed up to five hits to return a ball over the net; individual players are allowed two consecutive hits.

Regulation volleyball rules apply to rotating and scoring.

Beachball Volleyball

KEEP IT UP

Groups of 5-8 players are needed, each standing in a circle formation with one player assigned to start with the ball.

On a starting signal, the player with the ball tosses it up in the air. The players in the circle try to keep the ball up by striking it with legal volleyball hits. Each contact with the ball counts as a point. Players are to keep track of their highest consecutive string of hits.

The group has to start back at zero once the ball hits the floor or a player makes illegal contact with the ball. No player can hit the ball twice in succession. The group that ends up with the highest consecutive series of legal hits is declared the winner.

Keep It Up

NO RULES VOLLEYBALL

Well, there are some rules. However, this is a terrific game for your younger and/or less skilled students. To begin, one team serves from anywhere on the court. Members of the serving team can help the serve over the net with an unlimited number of assists. Teams and individuals are allowed an unlimited number of hits before a ball has to returned over the net. A ball must land on the opponent's court to score a point. Both the serving and receiving team can score. The team that reaches 15 points first wins.

No Rules Volleyball

NEWCOMB

Here's a game very much like regular volleyball except throwing and catching is used instead of volleyball striking. In fact, the objective is to throw the ball over the net so that it strikes the floor on the opponent's court, as well as to catch and send back any ball thrown by the opposing team.

The game begins with a serve (a thrown ball) by a designated team. Players on the receiving team try to catch it before it hits the floor. If so, the player making the catch has to throw from that spot. No walking with the ball is allowed and a player has only three seconds to throw it again. Play continues until one commits an error by failing to catch a thrown ball or a ball is thrown out of bounds.

Only the serving team score points. The first team to reach 15 points wins.

Newcomb

CATCH 22

Catch 22 allows multiple choices for players to send hit or send a volleyball over the net. Whenever a player has caught a ball (as in Newcomb above), he can send it back over the net or pass to a teammate by serving, throwing, setting, or bumping. The first team to reach 22 points wins. Otherwise, regulation volleyball rules apply.

This particular game allows the higher skilled player to use legal volleyball hits while, at the same time, it gives the less skilled player alternative methods of passing and scoring.

FOUR SQUARE VOLLEYBALL

Four Square Volleyball allows for large groups to all play at the same time. First, set up four nets with four equal teams on each of the four courts. Designate one team to start the game by serving into any other court. From then on, the game is played very much like regular volleyball. Each of the four teams attempt to hit the ball so that it lands on the court of another team. A point is given to a team whenever a ball lands on their side or they commit a volleyball rule violation. At the end of the playing period, the team with the lowest score wins.

For extra excitement and ball contact opportunities, consider adding an additional ball so that two balls are being played simultaneously.

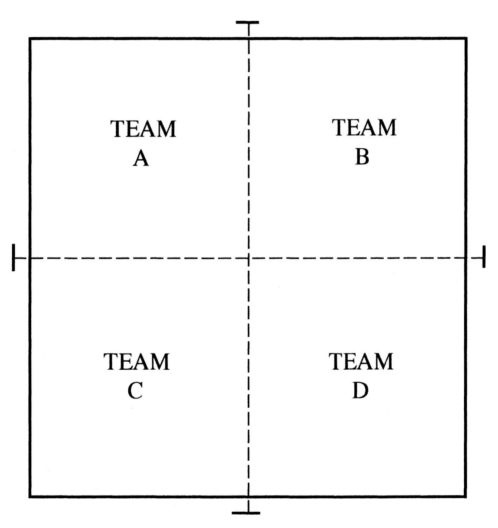

Four Square Volleyball

CHAPTER THREE

LARGE & SMALL GROUP GAMES

This chapter covers a variety of small and large group games that are ideal for the recess and playground setting. Through the use of game playing, children learn valuable physical, emotional, and cognitive skills in a meaningful setting. These games will keep your students actively participating during recess and will be fun for all involved.

BAMBOOZLE 'EM

WHERE TO PLAY: Anywhere
NUMBER OF PLAYERS: An entire class
SUGGESTED GRADE LEVELS: K-3rd grades
EQUIPMENT: Pinnies; football flags; a small object such as a key or coin

HOW TO PLAY: Divide the students into two equal teams with one team on each end line. Players should wear pinnies and have one flag hanging from a belt or back pocket.

One team starts first by huddling around the game leader, who places a small object into the hands of one of the players. Each of the huddled players closes his hands as if he holding the object. The huddled players then yell out "Go" and run toward the opponent's end line. The objective is for the player with the concealed object to score a touchdown by making it across the end line without getting his flag pulled. Since the defensive players do not know who has the object and who doesn't, they attempt to pull everyone's flag in order to catch the player with the coin. An offensive player must stop running and open his hands upon having his flag pulled.

Teams switch roles after each play. A touchdown counts as one point.

Bamboozle 'em

CAPTURE THE FLAG

WHERE TO PLAY: Outdoors
NUMBER OF PLAYERS: An entire class
SUGGESTED GRADE LEVELS: 3rd-8th grades
EQUIPMENT: Cones (for marking boundary lines); 6 hula hoops; 4 long ropes (for marking the jail and flag areas); 2 flags; and football flag sets for each player.

HOW TO PLAY: A playing area that is about 50' by 50' is ideal. A center line to divide the teams should also be established. With the ropes, mark off the corners for the two jails and flag spots. Three hula hoops are randomly placed on each side.

Divide the players into two equal teams. The players are to line up facing each other at the center line. All players are to wear two football flags.

On a starting signal, each team can rush across the center line attempting to capture the other team's flag. To be successful, a player has to carry the opponent's flag back to his own side without getting one of his football flags pulled. A player who at anytime is on the opposing team's side and has his football flag pulled must go to that team's jail. A jailed player can be freed if a teammate makes it into the prison (without getting his flag pulled), takes the prisoner by the hand and walks him back across the center line.

The hula hoops represent safety circles where players can stop off and not be tagged.
Only one player can be in a safety circle at any given time.

The first team to have both flags on their side wins the game.

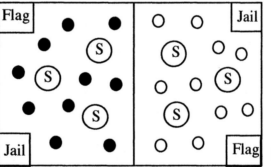 Capture the Flag

CROWS AND CRANES

WHERE TO PLAY: Anywhere
NUMBER OF PLAYERS: Unlimited

(continued on next page)

Crows and Cranes (cont.)

SUGGESTED GRADE LEVELS: K-4th grades
EQUIPMENT: None

HOW TO PLAY: Divide the players into two equal groups with the teams standing in a line (about 3'-5' apart) facing each other. One team is called the Crows, the other team the Cranes. A safety boundary line is about 30'- 40' behind each team.

On a starting signal, the game leader calls out either "Crows" or "Cranes." The players on the called team must run as fast as possible back to their safety line without being tagged by players on the opposite team. Since players will never know which team will be called, all should be anticipating to either run or chase. Each tagged player becomes a member of the opposite team. Players start back at the center lines at the conclusion of each play. Continue until all players on one of the teams have been caught.

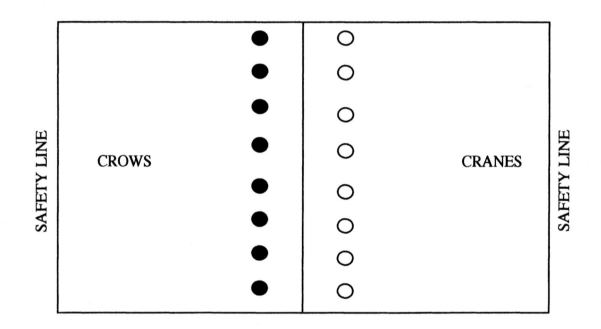

Crows and Cranes

DOCTOR DODGEBALL

WHERE TO PLAY: Gymnasium or outside
NUMBER OF PLAYERS: An entire class
SUGGESTED GRADE LEVELS: 1st-6th grades

EQUIPMENT: Enough foam balls for about half the number of players; two plastic baseball bats

HOW TO PLAY: If inside, use the basketball court lines for boundaries. For outside play, mark off a rectangular shaped playing area with a center line. Divide the players into two equally numbered teams, and have each team stand on their half of the playing area. One player from each team is designated as the "Doctor." The Doctor holds a plastic baseball bat (the "healing stick") which he will use to free his teammates during the game.

The objective is to hit all the opposing players and/or the opponent's doctor (with the soft foam balls) to win the game. The game begins with players throwing any balls that lie on their side of the playing area at the opposing players. Once a player is hit, he must lie on the ground pretending to be injured. The Doctor can "heal" (and allow him to participate again) this person if he touches him with his bat. No one can rescue the Doctor if he gets hit with a ball. The game ends when the Doctor is hit, or if one team successfully hits all the opponents. Change Doctors with each round of play.

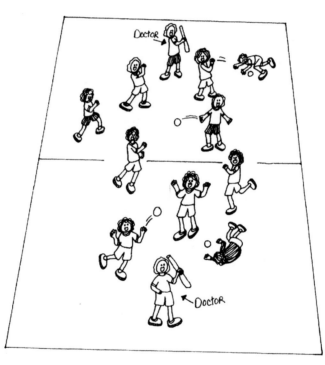

Doctor Dodgeball

END BALL

WHERE TO PLAY: Gym or outdoors
NUMBER OF PLAYERS: 10-30 players is ideal
SUGGESTED GRADE LEVELS: 3rd -8th grades
EQUIPMENT: 1-8 foam footballs

(continued on next page)

End Ball (cont.)

HOW TO PLAY: A basketball sized playing area is ideal. Divide the players into two equal teams. Each team needs to have half its players stationed behind its end line and the other half on their designated side of the playing area. The object of the game is to throw a foam football past the opponents and have it caught by a team member behind the end line.

The game begins with one team in possession of the ball. A point is scored each time a player successfully throws a football and has it caught by a teammate behind the end line. Only catches made by the end line players count as points. End line players throw the football back to their teammates after each completed and incompleted catch attempts. The defensive players (the players without the football) can knock down or intercept any pass made by the offensive team.

A football that goes out of bounds past the sidelines can be retrieved and put back into play by the nearest player to it. Players are required to stay in their designated areas throughout the game unless the game leader calls for a position switch. The team at the end of play with the highest point total wins the game.

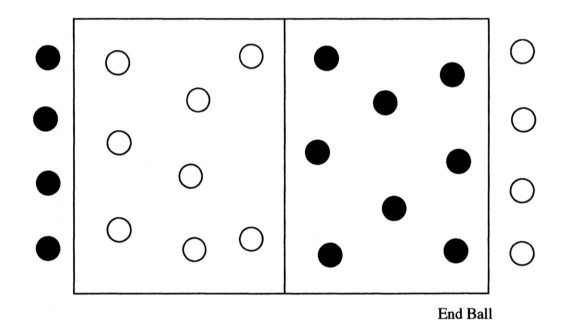

End Ball

FLICKERBALL

WHERE TO PLAY: Best played on a basketball court, inside or outside.
NUMBER OF PLAYERS: An entire class
SUGGESTED GRADE LEVELS: 3rd-8th grades
EQUIPMENT: One football; pinnies for each player
HOW TO PLAY: Divide the players into two equal teams with each team wearing pinnies. The

game begins with a team passing and advancing the football toward their basketball goal. Offensive players can try to score by either throwing the ball through the hoop (two points), or by hitting the backboard (one point). Players are allowed only three steps before passing, and no player can hold on to the football for more than five seconds. Either one of these violations will result in the other team gaining possession at that spot.

Defensive players are to guard the offensive players as in basketball. No touching is allowed. Defensive players can intercept passes, thus regaining possession for themselves.

Play for a predetermined time period. The team with the highest point total wins.

Flickerball

HILL DILL

WHERE TO PLAY: Anywhere
NUMBER OF PLAYERS: Unlimited
SUGGESTED GRADE LEVELS: K-4th grades
EQUIPMENT: None

(continued on next page)

Hill Dill (cont.)

HOW TO PLAY: Select one player to be "It" and stand in the middle of the playing area facing the lined players. The game begins with the "It" chanting, "Hill Dill come over the hill. I'll catch you if you're standing still." The players attempt to run to other side of the playing area while the "It" tries to tag as many as possible. Tagged players join the "It" at the center area and become helpers for the next round. Repeat until almost the entire group has become helpers.

LITTLE BROWN BEAR

WHERE TO PLAY: Gym or outside
NUMBER OF PLAYERS: Unlimited
SUGGESTED GRADE LEVELS: K-2nd grades
EQUIPMENT: None

HOW TO PLAY: Establish a playing area that is rectangular in shape with sidelines that are 30'-50' apart is ideal. Select one player to stand in the middle and start as the "Little Brown Bear." The other players are to line up on a sideline and face the Little Brown Bear.

The game begins with the Little Brown Bear calling out, "Who's afraid of the Little Brown Bear?" The other players respond with, "Not I." The Little Brown Bear then says "Then I want you to skip to the other side!" The players then must skip to other sideline (where they are safe) while the Little Brown bear attempts to tag them. Tagged players become helpers and join the Little Brown Bear in the middle. Helpers (and the Little Brown Bear) must travel the same way as the fleeing players. The little Brown Bear should call out a different way to travel each time (galloping, running, hopping, etc.) The game ends when all the players have been caught.

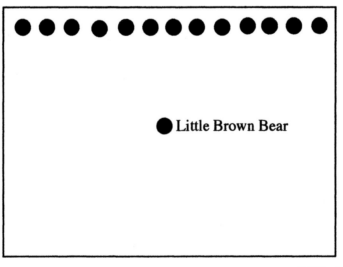

Little Brown Bear

MAN FROM MARS

WHERE TO PLAY: Anywhere
NUMBER OF PLAYERS: Unlimited
SUGGESTED GRADE LEVELS: K-2nd grades
EQUIPMENT: None

HOW TO PLAY: Select one player (the "Man from Mars") to stand in the middle of the playing area facing the lined players (the "earthlings"). The game begins with the earthlings chanting, "Man from Mars, Man from Mars. Will you take us to the stars?" The Man from Mars then replies, "Only if you are wearing_____(a color)." The earthlings with that colored clothing on may walk safely to the other side. Those without that color run to the side and try avoiding getting tagged. Tagged players join the Man from Mars in the center of the playing area.

MAT BALL

WHERE TO PLAY: Best played in a gymnasium
NUMBER OF PLAYERS: An entire class
SUGGESTED GRADE LEVELS: 3rd-8th grades
EQUIPMENT: Three tumbling mats; one home base; one foam soccer ball.

HOW TO PLAY: Set up the bases much like a softball field with a home base and tumbling mats for first, second and third bases. Divide the class into two equal teams with one team kicking first and the other in fielding positions.

This game is played like regular kickball with the following exceptions:
1) Baserunners have to circle the bases twice to score a run. They can stop on any base except home base.
2) An unlimited number of baserunners can be on first, second, and third bases. Baserunners do not have to run on a kicked ball at any time. Because of this, there are no force-outs.
3) There is no leading-off or stealing allowed for baserunners. They must stay on a base until the ball has been kicked.
4) Each kicker is allowed only one rolled pitch. A foul kick results in an out.
5) Teams switch places after 5 outs.

There are three ways of getting a kicker/baserunner out. They include: catching a fly ball; tagging a baserunner while off a base; throwing and hitting the baserunner with the ball below the waist.

One point is awarded for each baserunner that successfully circles the bases twice. The team with the highest point total wins. (continued on next page)

Mat Ball

PIN BALL

WHERE TO PLAY: A gym is ideal, but can be played outside on pavement.
NUMBER OF PLAYERS: An entire class
SUGGESTED GRADE LEVELS: 2nd-8th grades
EQUIPMENT: 6-8 cones; 6-8 plastic balls; 8-10 foam soccer balls

HOW TO PLAY: Set up a playing area as shown below with plastic balls placed on top of 3-4 cones on the end lines. Each team begins with 4-5 soft soccer balls. The objective is to be the first team to knock the plastic balls off all the opponent's cones or to hit all the opponents with a rolled ball.

On a starting signal, players begin rolling the foam soccer balls at the opponents or their cones. Players have to stay on their half of the playing area at all times unless they are hit with a rolled ball. If hit, the player crosses over and joins the opposing team.

When a plastic ball is knocked off a cone, it can not be replaced. A team wins when it has successfully knocked off all their opponent's plastic balls or if they have hit all their opponents within a rolled ball.

Pin Ball

PRISONERS DODGEBALL

WHERE TO PLAY: Either outside or in a gymnasium
NUMBER OF PLAYERS: Up to 30 students is ideal
SUGGESTED GRADE LEVELS: 2nd-8th grades
EQUIPMENT: 5-15 foam balls; 2-4 long jump ropes

HOW TO PLAY: Players are divided into two equal teams with each team standing on their half of the playing area. If inside, a basketball court works great as a playing area. If outside, use cone markers for a 30' x 40' size playing area as well as the center line. Use the long jump ropes to mark off a prison area at the far end of each side.

Start with several foam balls (but add more as the game goes on). Players throw the foam ball back and forth at each other, attempting to hit an opponent below the waist. If hit, a player goes to the opponent's prison. A player also goes to prison if his thrown ball is caught on the fly by an opponent.

A prisoner can be freed by picking up any ball that rolls or bounces into the prison, and hitting an opponent with it. The prisoner is then released and the hit player goes to the prison on the other side. Teammates can also help out prisoners if they throw a ball into the prison so that it can be caught on the fly. When this happens, the prisoner catching the ball is free without having to hit an opponent. Opponents can not enter a prison to go after a ball. (continued on next page)

Prisoners Dodgeball (cont.)

The game ends when one team has secured all the players from the other team in their prison or if one team ends up with more prisoners at the end of the playing time.

Prisoners Dodgeball

RED LIGHT - GREEN LIGHT

WHERE TO PLAY: Anywhere
NUMBER OF PLAYERS: An entire class
SUGGESTED GRADE LEVELS: K-2nd grades
EQUIPMENT: None

HOW TO PLAY: Select one player to be the "traffic light;" he is to stand 30'- 60' away from the other players who are lined up facing him.

The game begins with traffic light player turning his back to the line players and yelling out "Green Light." The line players can walk or run toward the traffic light player; however, at any time, the traffic light player can yell out "Red Light," and turn around. The line players must stop immediately. Any player caught still moving must go back to the starting line. Players not caught are allowed to stay where they are. Play continues in this fashion until one of the players finally touches the traffic light. The winning player becomes the traffic light for the next round.

SACK THE QUARTERBACK

WHERE TO PLAY: Anywhere
NUMBER OF PLAYERS: An entire class
SUGGESTED GRADE LEVELS: 2nd-6th grades
EQUIPMENT: Flags for each player

HOW TO PLAY: All players need to wear flags (hanging from a belt or back pocket). Select two players (the "sackers") to stand in a center circle. The other players (the "Quarterbacks") start by standing around the circle that contains the two sackers. The Quarterbacks begin by slowly edging closer and closer to the sackers until the sackers (at any time) yell out "Sack." At that time, the sackers attempt to pull the Quarterbacks flags as they flee to one of the four boundary lines. Once a Quarterback crosses a line he is safe. If a Quarterback does have his flag pulled, he becomes a sacker helper and joins them each time in the center circle. The game continues until there are very few Quarterbacks left.

Sack The Quarterback

SPUD

WHERE TO PLAY: Anywhere
NUMBER OF PLAYERS: Unlimited
SUGGESTED GRADE LEVELS: 2nd-6th grades
EQUIPMENT: One foam ball

HOW TO PLAY: Have the players stand in a circle facing the center player who is holding the ball. Before starting, each of the players should have an assigned number.

(continued on next page)

Spud (cont.)

The game starts with the circle players jogging clockwise around the center player. At any time, the center player can toss the ball up into the air and call out a number. The player whose number is called attempts to catch the ball by the second bounce, and yells "Freeze" to the fleeing circle players. All the players must then stay motionless in their positions. The player with the ball is allowed up to three steps toward a player in order to hit him below the waist. If successful, the thrower becomes the circle player for the next round. If unsuccessful, the game starts again with the original center player. Play is continuous.

Spud

SQUIRRELS IN THE TREES

WHERE TO PLAY: Anywhere
NUMBER OF PLAYERS: Unlimited
SUGGESTED GRADE LEVELS: K-3rd grades
EQUIPMENT: None

HOW TO PLAY: Have the players form trees by two players facing each other with hands on each other's shoulders. A third player (the "squirrel") stands in the middle of each tree. One or two extra squirrels without trees are needed before beginning the game. On a signal, the squirrels have to move out of their trees to another while, at the same time, the extra squirrels hurriedly attempt to find a tree. Only one squirrel is allowed in each tree and a squirrel can not return to a tree where he had been previously. The objective for the squirrels is to never be left out.

So that the tree players have chances at being squirrels, design a system of rotation whereby when the squirrel moves into a tree, he changes places with one of the tree players.

Squirrels in the Trees

STEAL THE BEANBAGS

WHERE TO PLAY: Can be played outside or in a gymnasium
NUMBER OF PLAYERS: An entire class
SUGGESTED GRADE LEVELS: 3rd-8th grades
EQUIPMENT: Twenty beanbags; two hula hoops; flag sets for each player

HOW TO PLAY: This is a great game that will keep kids continuously active for long periods of time. Because of the higher level of physical activity, it is also a more attractive alternative to the traditional (but largely sedentary) game of Steal The Bacon.

Mark off a playing area that is about 20 by 30 yards in size (or the size of a basketball court if inside), with a center dividing line. Place a hula hoop, each containing 10 beanbags in the center, at the far end of each side. Divide the players into two equal teams, with each team wearing colored flags (for pulling). Players are to start the game on their half of the field.

The objective is to be the first team to have all twenty beanbags inside their own hula hoop. However, this rarely happens. The game will sometimes go on for an hour!

On a starting signal, team members can cross the center dividing line trying to steal the opponents'

(continued on next page)

Steal the Beanbags (cont.)

beanbags. However, once a player crosses over into the opponent's side, he can have his flag pulled. If this happens, the player with the pulled flag must stand in a frozen position, and the player who pulled it places the flag on the center line. This frozen player can be freed if a team member picks up the flag and runs it to him (provided he doesn't get tagged as well). Both players hold on to the flag and walk back to their side (no one can pull their flags in this position). The rescued player reattaches his flag and now is allowed to play again.

A player is allowed to pick up only one beanbag at a time. Players are not allowed to make hand-offs, pass a beanbag, or kick a beanbag while attempting to run back with it.

A player who has his flagged pulled must return the beanbag.

An area around the hula hoop can be designated as an off-limits territory for team members guarding the beanbags. This will prevent defensive players from bunching up around the hoop.

This never ending game is sure to become one of your school's favorites!

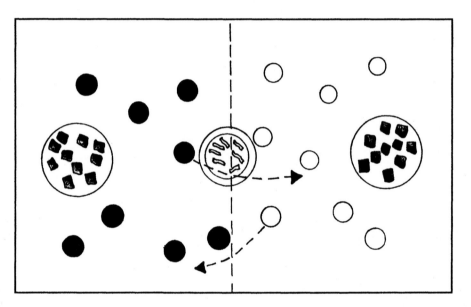

Steal The Beanbags

TAG GAMES

WHERE TO PLAY: Depends on the specific tag gam; however, most can be played anywhere.

NUMBER OF PLAYERS: Most tag games will need to have at least several players.
An entire class can participate in most games.

SUGGESTED GRADE LEVELS: K-8th grades

EQUIPMENT: Most tag games involve taggers, so pinnies, balls, etc. are often used to tell them apart. Equipment may also be used (dribbling and catching a ball for example) as part of the movement required.

HOW TO PLAY: Since there are many forms of tag, see the specific rules for each game.

SPECIAL NOTE: Always be sure to instruct the players to run and move safely during these games to avoid injury. Jogging, skipping, etc., would be more appropriate traveling options for the younger players. Avoid playing these games around any object(s) that players could run into and be injured.

Tag

BLOB TAG

One of my students' favorite games! Select two players to hold hands and be the "blob." The other players scatter throughout the playing area. The "blob" chases other players attempting to tag them with their outside hands. Tagged players hold hands with the blob and become part of the growing blob. The blob can never break up--it just keeps getting larger and larger until everyone is caught.

MINI-BLOB TAG

Played exactly like Blob Tag (see previous game) except the blob breaks up in pairs when it has four players. Subsequent blobs will do the same. As in regular Blob Tag, the blobs must hold hands and attempt to tag others with their outside hands. Because of the increased and growing number of blobs, this game will end much sooner than regular Blob Tag. This is a great game with a lot of running and movement.

STUCK IN THE MUD

Another continuous running game with lots of fun action. Designate 3-6 players to be the "Its," each wearing pinnies or holding foam balls (to tag others with).

The game begins with the "Its" chasing others, attempting to tag everyone in order to end the game. Tagged players must stand with their feet apart, hands on top of their heads. The remaining free players can free the tagged players by crawling between their legs.

HIT THE DECK TAG

Designate 3-6 players to be the "Its," each holding a small foam ball (for tagging others). The "Its" begin by chasing the other players, attempting to tag everyone and stop the game. At anytime, players can avoid being tagged by lying on their backs with arms and legs pointing upward. Upside down players can start running again at anytime.

Players that are tagged must lie on their stomachs. Free players can touch tagged players, thereby allowing them to play again. Lots of continuous action.

LINE TAG

This game is best played on a basketball court (inside or outside). Have the players stand on the court lines. Select three players to be taggers. Each should have a small foam ball in his hands. On a starting signal, the taggers chase the others attempting to touch another player with his ball (no throwing allowed). Once a player is tagged, he takes the ball and becomes one of the taggers. All players, including the taggers, must stay on the lines. At the end of play, the players who have been the taggers the least often can be designated the game champions. Another game with lots of continuous action.

ELBOW TAG

With the exception of 1-3 players (who start the game as "Its"), have the players pair up and stand with elbows locked together. The paired partners have their outside hands on their hips. On a starting signal, each of the "Its" chase and try to hook on to the outside elbow of a free player. If successful, the player on the other side is forced to let go and become an "It." Play is continuous.

BRIDGE TAG

Depending on the number of participants, select 2-4 "Its." When a player is tagged, he makes a bridge by going down to the ground on his hands and feet. A tagged player has to stay in this position until a free player crawls through his bridge. This is a continuous action game that doesn't end unless all of the players are frozen or time has been called.

SQUAT TAG

Select three players to be "Its," each holding a small foam ball with which to tag others. This game is played like most other tag games except that players are safe from being tagged by assuming a squatting position with both hands on the floor. A limit of 1-3 "squats" is usually implemented to prevent overuse of the procedure. A player that is tagged takes the ball and becomes an "It."

BEANBAG TAG

Each player starts with a beanbag. The object of the game is to tag others by hitting their feet (or shoes) with an underhanded throw; and, because everyone is an "It", to avoid being tagged. Once tagged, a player must perform 10 jumping jacks (or similar activity) before being allowed back into the game. Continuous action.

NORTH WIND - SOUTH WIND

Start with three players designated as the North Wind players (the chasers) and one player as the South Wind player (the unfreezer). The North Wind players chase and try to tag as many players as possible. If tagged, a player must go down on all fours (hands and feet). The only way a tagged player can become free again is to have the South Wind player tag him while he's in the frozen position. The North Wind players cannot tag the South Wind player. Play is continuous.

SPORTS TAG

Start with three taggers who have a foam ball in their hands (to distinguish themselves as the taggers). On a starting signal, the taggers attempt to tag as many players as possible. If tagged, a player must assume a sports stance or position (such as a baseball player in a batting stance or a basketball player shooting, etc.). A tagged player can play again only if a free player comes up to him and guesses the correct sport. If the free player guesses incorrectly, the tagged player must stay in that position until another player ultimately guesses the correct sport. Play is continuous.

LAUGH TAG

Start with three taggers. On a starting signal, the taggers attempt to tag as many players as possible. If tagged, a player puts his hands on his hips and stands with a sad look on his face. However, a tagged player can play again if a free player comes up to him and makes a funny face which causes him to smile and/or laugh. Play is continuous.

GERM TAG

Start with 3-5 players each holding a foam ball (the germs). On a starting signal, the players with the germs (the balls) each attempt to tag another player. A tagged player takes the ball and becomes the new tagger. The newly tagged player then quickly tries to tag another player with it so he doesn't have to hold on to the "germ." Play for a predetermined time period with the players tagged the least often the winners.

CIRCLE TAG

Divide the players into four-player groups. Three of the players join hands to make a circle. One player stands outside the circle and is the tagger. The tagger names one of the circle players that he will attempt to touch.

The tagger has to go around the outside of the circle to touch the named player. He can not reach across the middle. The circle players move either clockwise or counterclockwise to help the player from being tagged. However, the circle players must stay in the same spot (that is, the circle can't move all around the playing area). Once the tagger is successful, he switches places and joins the circle. Play continues again with the tagger calling out the name of the next player to be chased.

FREEZE TAG

Choose three players to be taggers (the freezers) and two players (the defrosters) to free others. The taggers attempt to freeze all the players while, at the same time, the defrosters touch the frozen players and free them. The defrosters have to avoid the taggers as they can become frozen as well. Play is continuous until all the players are frozen.

EVERYONE'S IT

As the name of this game implies, everyone is an "It." On a starting signal, everyone tries to tag as many other players as possible while, at the same time, avoiding being tagged themselves. The players are to keep a running count of the number of players they are able to tag. At the end of a predetermined time limit (1-2 minutes), stop the game. The player with the highest number of tags wins the contest.

CABOOSE TAG

With the exception of three players (the "Its"), form groups (the "trains") of four or five players with each standing in a file. Hands should be on the hips of the person in front of them. On a starting

94

signal, the "trains" are free to run anywhere, as long as they do not break apart. Each "It" attempts to catch up with a "train" and attach itself to the end. If successful, the caboose yells out "new caboose," resulting in the front player now becoming an "It". "Its" have to find a new "train" on which to attach. Continual play.

SPOT TAG

Designate three "Its" with the other players scattered throughout the playing area. When a player is tagged, he has to grab the spot where he was tagged with one hand (but is still allowed to be chased). When tagged a second time, the player uses his other hand to touch the spot where he was tagged (but he is still be chased). When tagged a third time, he becomes a tagger himself. The game ends when all players have become taggers.

WALL TUNNEL TAG

This tag game is best played in a gymnasium or a covered play area that has walls. Select three taggers. The taggers will attempt to tag as many players as possible. If tagged, a player must go over to a wall, put his feet on the wall and support himself with his hands. He must stay in this position until a free player crawls through his "tunnel." Play is continuous.

PARTNER TAG

Have the players pair up with a partner and hold hands. Assign 1-3 couples to start the game as taggers. They should hold a foam ball to identify themselves. On a starting signal, each of the tag couples attempt to touch other couples with their ball. If tagged, a couple takes the ball and become the new chasers. Play for a set time limit. At the end, the couples that have been the taggers the least often can be declared the champs.

ANIMAL TAG

A playing area with two parallel lines about 30'-50' is ideal. Divide the players into two equal groups with each group standing on a sideline. The game leader goes to one group and they quietly decide on a particular animal they would like to imitate. This group then moves like that animal all the way over to within 5'- 6' of the other group. The group watching now tries to guess which animal they were imitating. If they guess correctly, they chase the first group back to its line, attempting to tag as many as possible. If tagged, a player must join that team. The groups then reverse roles and alternate this pattern throughout the game.

SUNDAY

WHERE TO PLAY: Anywhere
NUMBER OF PLAYERS: Unlimited
SUGGESTED GRADE LEVELS: K-3rd grades
EQUIPMENT: None

HOW TO PLAY: A playing area that has two parallel lines about 30'-60' apart is ideal. Assign one player to be the tagger and to stand in the middle. The other players start by standing on one of the sidelines.

The line players must run across to the other sideline every time the tagger calls out "Sunday." The tagger will attempt to catch as many players as possible. If caught, a player joins the tagger in the middle and becomes his helper.

The tagger can also call out any other day of the week. If a line player starts running prematurely on any day except Sunday, he has to join the tagger in the middle. The game ends when all the line players have been caught.

TREES

WHERE TO PLAY: Gym or outside; a rectangular shaped playing area with sidelines about 30'-50' apart is ideal.
NUMBER OF PLAYERS: Unlimited
SUGGESTED GRADE LEVELS: K-4th grades
EQUIPMENT: None

HOW TO PLAY: One player is selected to be the "It" and stands in the middle; the other players lined up along a sideline. When the "It" yells out "Trees," the players run to the other sideline with the "It" attempting to tag as many as possible. Once on the sideline, a player is safe. If tagged, a player becomes a tree (and a helper) and must stand exactly at the spot where tagged. A tree can not run, but he can tag others who run by close enough. The game continues in this fashion until all the players have become trees.

This game is sometimes even more fun, and much faster, with two taggers instead of just one.

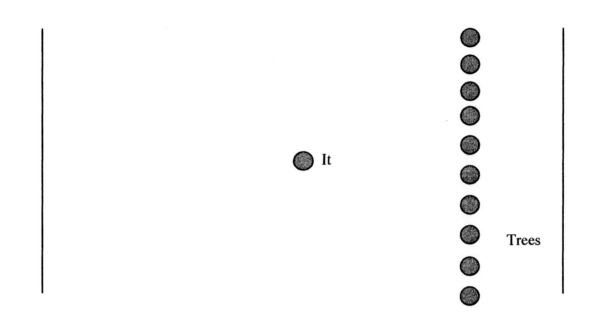

It

Trees

TRUTH OR CONSEQUENCES

WHERE TO PLAY: Outside or in a gymnasium
NUMBER OF PLAYERS: An entire class
SUGGESTED GRADE LEVELS: 1st-6th grades
EQUIPMENT: None

HOW TO PLAY: This activity is played very much like Crows and Cranes, but the cognitive challenges of this version will be more appealing to older student.

Divide the players into two equal groups, with the teams facing each other about 3-5 feet apart. Have the students come up with team names, such as "Bulls" and "Bears." Mark off a safety boundary line about 30-40 feet behind each team.

The game begins with the game leader calling out a statement that is either unmistakingly true or clearly false. The game leader can use math facts, word spelling, geography facts, or even simple statements such as "The name of our school is... ." If the statement is true, the Bulls chase the Bears back to their safety line. If false, the Bears chase the Bulls. Any player who is tagged becomes a member of the opposing team. Players start back at the center area at the conclusion of each play. Continue until all the players on one of the teams have been caught.

ULTIMATE FRISBEE

WHERE TO PLAY: Outside on a soccer or football sized field.
NUMBER OF PLAYERS: At least 6 players
SUGGESTED GRADE LEVELS: 3rd-8th grades
EQUIPMENT: One frisbee; and pinnies to identify teams

HOW TO PLAY: Form two equal teams, with each team standing on their own goal line. Designate one team to start with the frisbee first.

The game begins with the offensive team (the team with the frisbee) advancing the frisbee down the field by throwing and catching the frisbee to teammates. Players in possession of the frisbee can not walk or run with it; however, a player can pivot on one foot (as in basketball) while trying to pass. Players that do walk or run with the frisbee forfeit possession to the other team.

The defensive team can intercept the frisbee at any time. Also, if an offensive team allows the frisbee to fall uncaught to the ground, the other team is given possession. Defensive players can guard but cannot touch or make physical contact with the offensive players. If so, a non-guarded free throw is made at the spot of the infraction.

To score, the offensive team must have the frisbee caught by one of its' players behind the opponent's goal line. Each goal counts as one point. After each score, the teams line up again on their goal lines and the non-scoring team starts with possession of the frisbee.

Play usually continues until a predetermined number of points has been reached or a time limit has been met.

Ultimate Frisbee

CHAPTER FOUR

RELAY GAMES

   Relay activities are a wonderful teaching tool for introducing children to the importance of group participation and cooperation in reaching a desired goal. This chapter covers a variety of relay activities that will help children learn to cooperate with others, enhance movement skills, and develop endurance and fitness.

BALL RELAYS

WHERE TO PLAY: Anywhere
NUMBER OF PLAYERS: 4-6 players to a team; unlimited teams
SUGGESTED GRADE LEVELS: K-8th grades
EQUIPMENT: One playground ball for each team

HOW TO PLAY: Divide the players into teams of 4-6 players each. Each team starts with one ball. As in most relays, the objective is to be the first team to complete the required tasks. The following are specific relays using a ball.

DRIBBLE & HOP

Each team lines up in file with the first player holding the ball. On a starting signal, the first player from each team runs and dribbles his ball to a turn-a-round cone. Once there, he puts the ball between his ankles and hops back to the starting line. The subsequent players do the same. First team to complete the relay wins.

Dribble & Hop

OVER 'N' UNDER

Each team is to stand in a file with each player about 2-3 feet behind the player in front. On a starting signal, the first player passes the ball to the player behind him by handing it straight over the top of his head. The receiving player passes the ball to the next player by going between his legs with it. This "over and under" pattern continues until the last player receives the ball. At that time, the receiver takes the ball, runs to the beginning of the line and starts the over and under pattern again. The relay ends when all the players are back in their original positions.

Over 'N' Under

PASS 'N' DUCK

Teams are to start with one player (the leader) holding a ball and facing their teammates who are standing in a file (about 10' away). On a starting signal, the leader passes the ball to the first teammate in line. This player catches the ball, passes it back to the leader and squats down. The leader then passes the ball to the next player, and so on. The last player receiving the ball takes the place of the leader who runs to the beginning of the line. Play continues in this pattern until all players are back into their original positions.

Pass 'N' Duck

DRIBBLE, PIVOT & PASS

Designate a starting line and a pivoting line that are about 5'-10' apart. Teams start in a file formation. The first player in line dribbles to the pivoting line, performs a basketball pivot and passes the ball to the next teammate who does the same. The relay ends when all the players are back in their original positions.

(continued on next page)

Dribble, Pivot & Pass

CONTINUOUS PASSING RELAY

Players stand side by side in a straight line with one player (the leader) positioned about 5-10 feet away holding the ball and facing his teammates. On a starting signal, the leader passes the ball to the first player on the left side, who catches the ball and passes it right back to the leader. The leader does the same with the next player, and so on. The last player receiving a pass runs forward and becomes the new leader. The leader becomes the first player on the left side. The relay ends when all the players are back in their starting positions.

BASERUNNING RELAY

WHERE TO PLAY: A softball diamond; if not available, place four bases in an infield formation.
NUMBER OF PLAYERS: Four teams of equal numbered players
SUGGESTED GRADE LEVELS: 2nd-8th grades
EQUIPMENT: Bases

HOW TO PLAY: Place each of the four teams at a base. On a starting signal, the first player in each team runs counterclockwise around the bases, touching each one. When he gets back to his starting base, he tags the next teammate in line and goes to the back of the line. The relay ends when all the players have run the bases. The first team that completes the relay wins.

Consider moving the bases further apart to add distance to the running.

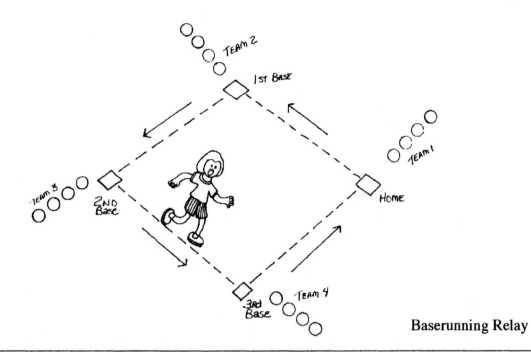

Baserunning Relay

BEANBAG RELAY

WHERE TO PLAY: Anywhere
NUMBER OF PLAYERS: 3-5 players to a team; unlimited teams
SUGGESTED GRADE LEVELS: K-8th grades
EQUIPMENT: Three hula hoops, three bean bags, and one box for each team

HOW TO PLAY: The teams start by standing in a file formation behind a box (which contains three bean bags). Three hula hoops are to be placed about 10' apart in a straight line in front of each team.

(continued on next page)

Beanbag Relay

Beanbag Relay (cont.)

On a starting signal, the first player in each team takes one bean bag from their box and puts it into the first hula hoop. This same player then takes another bean bag, places it inside the second hula hoop, and does the same for the third hula hoop. When finished, the player tags the next teammate in line who then picks up the bean bag in the first hula hoop, brings it back to the box, and continues in this same fashion. The relay ends when each player has had a turn.

CROSS COUNTRY RELAY

WHERE TO PLAY: Outside
NUMBER OF PLAYERS: Four players to a team; unlimited teams
SUGGESTED GRADE LEVELS: 1st-8th grades
EQUIPMENT: None

HOW TO PLAY: Mark off a 200-400 meter running course or a distance which is appropriate for the age of the players. Divide the players into equal teams of 4-5 players.

On a starting signal, all of the players begin running. The objective is for each player to run as many completed laps as possible within a predetermined time limit. While running, each player is responsible for counting the number of laps completed. After the race, the players add up the number of completed laps as a team. The team with the highest number wins.

Cross Country Relay

COOPERATIVE RELAYS

WHERE TO PLAY: Outside if possible
NUMBER OF PLAYERS: 4-6 players to a group; unlimited groups
SUGGESTED GRADE LEVELS: K-8th grades
EQUIPMENT: Cones

HOW TO PLAY: Each group will position itself behind a starting cone. Depending on the specific relay event (see specific relays below), each group performs the required task down to the turn-a-round cone and back. The first team back to the starting line wins.

CHARIOTS OF FIRE

Each team begin by having all its players facing outward and holding hands except the "chariot driver," who is at the back of the circle, facing inward and holding hands. Teams can not break hands at anytime while running. Play several times giving others an opportunity to be the driver.

Chariots of Fire

SEDAN RELAY

Start with one player to be carried, two players to carry and one or two players in relief who can switch off with the two carriers when they tire. The sedan is formed with the two carriers facing each other and grasping hands with each other. The carrier sits on the hands and puts his hands around the neck and shoulders of the carriers.

This is a very tiring event for the carriers. Have the players rotate positions (including any relief players) after a certain distance.

(continued on next page)

Sedan Relay

WHEELBARROW RELAY

Have the players pair up with a teammate. One player starts in a "push-up" position. The second player grasps the partner's legs and holds his legs about waist high. On a starting signal, the first couple in each team will travel in a wheelbarrow position to the turnaround spot; at that time, the players switch positions, and travel back to the starting line. The next couple starts and does the same until everyone has had a turn. The first team to complete the relay wins.

Wheelbarrow Relay

MAN IN THE MOON

Teams line up holding hands in a circle with one player (the "Man on the Moon") standing in the middle. When running, the middle player must stay in the middle. After each completed turn, the teams exchange middle players and take off again. Continue until everyone has had a chance to be the Man on the Moon.

Man In The Moon

THE TRAIN

Have the players on each team hold on a long jump rope with one hand. The players cannot let go when running. After each completed turn, the player in front moves to the back and the team takes off again. Continue until everyone is back in their original starting position.

The Train

LEAP FROG RELAY

Begin with a starting line and a finishing line that's about 30'- 50' apart. Each team starts behind the starting line in a file formation. Players should be in a squatting position, several feet apart.

On a signal, the last player in line leapfrogs over each member of the team until he becomes the first person in line. The new last person now does the same. This players continue in this fashion until they reach the finish line.

(continued on next page)

Leap Frog Relay

MOVEMENT SKILL RELAYS

WHERE TO PLAY: Can be done anywhere, but best played outdoors on grass
NUMBER OF PLAYERS: 3-5 players to a team; unlimited teams
SUGGESTED GRADE LEVELS: K-8th grades
EQUIPMENT: Cones

HOW TO PLAY: Group the players into equal teams of 3-5 players. Each team starts by sitting in a file behind a starting cone. A turn-a-round cone is placed about 40'-100' in front of each team (distance will depend on the age of the players). On a starting signal, the first player in each team moves as quickly as possible down the field, around the cone and back to the starting line where he tags the next teammate in line. That player does the same and so on. A team sits down when all of its players have finished. The team finishing ahead of the others wins.
  Some of the movements that the game leader can call are:
- Running
- Running forward halfway; run backwards on the return
- Crab Walk (moving on hands and feet in an inverted position)
- Bear Walk (running on all fours)
- Skipping
- Galloping
- Backwards skipping
- Hop on one foot down; on other foot back
- Jump down; run back
- Slide down; leap back
- Any combination of the above (for example, skip down; run back)

Movement Skills Relay

PONY EXPRESS

WHERE TO PLAY: Outside
NUMBER OF PLAYERS: Four on a team is ideal; unlimited teams
SUGGESTED GRADE LEVELS: 2nd-8th grades
EQUIPMENT: Cones; an object to be exchanged such as batons, erasers, etc.

HOW TO PLAY: Mark off an oval shaped running area, much as a real track would look like. Place four cones along the running area, equally spaced apart. Form teams of four players each and assign a player from each team to one of the four spots. The first player (at station #1) starts with the baton (or similar object) to be handed off.

Pony Express

On a starting signal, the first runner from each team carries the baton to the teammate at station #2. After handing the baton off, runner #1 stays at station #2. Runner #2 runs to station #3, hands off the baton to the teammate there and stays at station #3. Play continues like this with Runner #4 carrying the baton two spaces to station #2. Every runner at station #4 will have to do this throughout the playing of the game. The race is finished when all the players are back in their original starting spots.

RESCUE RELAY

WHERE TO PLAY: Anywhere
NUMBER OF PLAYERS: 3-5 players on a team; unlimited teams
SUGGESTED GRADE LEVELS: K-6th grades
EQUIPMENT: Cones

HOW TO PLAY: Mark off two lines about 30'-60' apart. Teams line up in a file with the exception of one player who stands at the opposite line facing his teammates. On a starting signal, the single player from each team runs to the first teammate in line, grasps him by the wrist, and runs back to his line. The rescued player then runs back and gets the next player in line. The relay continues in this fashion until all have been rescued.

Rescue Relay

TRAVELING TASKS RELAY

WHERE TO PLAY: Inside or on pavement
NUMBER OF PLAYERS: 3-5 players on a team; unlimited teams
SUGGESTED GRADE LEVELS: K-8th grades
EQUIPMENT: Depends on the tasks required. The example below involves three hula hoops, one bean bag, one jump rope, and one basketball for each team.

HOW TO PLAY: Players line up in a file formation behind the starting line. Three hula hoops are placed about 15-30 feet apart in a straight line in front of each team. The first hula hoop contains a bean bag, the second has a jump rope, and the third contains a basketball.

On a starting signal, the first player from each team runs to the first hula hoop, picks up the bean bag, puts it on his head, and balances it while he walks/runs to the next hula hoop. At the second hula hoop, he puts the bean bag down, picks up the jump rope, and jumps rope (while he's moving) to the third hula hoop. There he puts the rope down, takes the basketball, and dribbles back to the first hula hoop. He puts the basketball inside the first hula hoop, runs back to his team, and tags the next player in line. That player does the same and play continues in this fashion until all the players have finished.

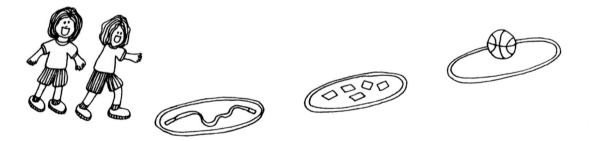

Traveling Tasks Relay

CHAPTER FIVE

CLASSROOM GAMES & ACTIVITIES

On many occasions, foul weather or unavailable space will result in recess and physical education needing to take place in the classroom. This chapter contains a variety of challenging indoor games and activities that can be used in the classroom. They require very little equipment, are easy to teach, and offer a fun alternative to the normal recess/physical education setting.

ALPHABETICAL NUMBERS

WHERE TO PLAY: Anywhere
NUMBER OF PLAYERS: 3 on up to an entire class
SUGGESTED GRADE LEVELS: 1st- 6th grades
EQUIPMENT: None

HOW TO PLAY: One player starts by standing in front of the others and calling out any number between 1 and 26. The other players try to be the first to find the corresponding letter of the alphabet (1 equals A, 2 equals B, etc.) The first player with the correct answer gets to be the next caller.

A variation of this game is to call out letters instead of numbers. Players must then guess the correct letter; A equals 1, Z equals 26, etc.

ANSWER SCRAMBLE

WHERE TO PLAY: In the classroom with a large open area, or outside
NUMBER OF PLAYERS: An entire class
SUGGESTED GRADE LEVELS: K-8th grades
EQUIPMENT: None

HOW TO PLAY: This is a great activity that combines creative movement with problem solving.

"what letter begins in volleyball?"

Answer Scramble

Divide the players into groups of 5-6 players each. Each group needs its own space within the room. The game leader stands in front of the room so that he can see all the groups. The game leader starts by calling out a number or letter that he wants the groups to assemble themselves in. For example, he might say "What letter begins in volleyball?" or "How many points wins a volleyball game?" The first team to most accurately form the number or letter (by using their bodies collectively as a group) scores one point. The team at the end of the playing time with the highest number of points wins

BACK TO BACK

WHERE TO PLAY: Anywhere
NUMBER OF PLAYERS: An entire class
SUGGESTED GRADE LEVELS: K-6th grades
EQUIPMENT: None

HOW TO PLAY: This is a fun icebreaker and getting acquainted game. With the exception of one player (the "It"), players begin by standing back-to-back with a partner.
The "It" starts out by calling a command with two body parts (an example would be "touch one elbow with your partner's elbow.") After several of these calls, the "It" says "Switch Partners." The players are to quickly find a new partner to stand back-to-back with. However, the "It," at the same time, tries to find a partner. This results in another player not having a partner and becoming the new "It." Play continues with the new "It" making the next set of commands and switching partners.
   Players cannot have the same partner twice during the game. This rule reinforces interaction with others.

Back To Back

BALLOON VOLLEYBALL

WHERE TO PLAY: Anywhere
NUMBER OF PLAYERS: Entire class
SUGGESTED GRADE LEVELS: 1st-8th grades
EQUIPMENT: 2-5 balloons; a rope or chalk

HOW TO PLAY: Divide the class into two equal teams, with all players seated on the floor. A line or rope should be placed, either on the floor or 2-3 feet off the floor, to separate the two teams. Players are to remain seated and can not stand at any time during the game

For the most fun, this game is best played informally without most of the rules and violations of regular volleyball. The players start by hitting a balloon back and forth across the line. A point can be scored only if the balloon touches the floor or wall on the opponent's side. The balloon can be batted an unlimited number of times by a player or team. After a few minutes, add a second balloon, then a third, etc., to add action and excitement to the contest.

Balloon Volleyball

BEANBAG RELAY

WHERE TO PLAY: Anywhere
NUMBER OF PLAYERS: 3-6 in each group; unlimited groups
SUGGESTED GRADE LEVELS: K-6th grades

EQUIPMENT: Five bean bags per group

HOW TO PLAY: Players are to stand in a column of equal numbers. The first person in each column starts with five beanbags. On a starting signal, the first player passes the bean bags over his shoulder to the second player in line. The second player must have all five bean bags in his possession before passing them to the third player, etc. When the last player has received all five bean bags, all the players in the line turn and face the opposite direction. The bean bags are then passed in the same manner as before. The first team to have its five bean bags returned to the player at the front of the line wins the contest.

Beanbag Relay

CHARADES

WHERE TO PLAY: Indoors or outdoors
NUMBER OF PLAYERS: Any number
GRADE LEVELS: 3rd-8th grade
EQUIPMENT: None

Charades

(continued on next page)

Charades (cont.)

HOW TO PLAY: Two teams are formed. One team starts as the actors and the other as the audience. The acting team decides on a famous saying, movie, person, etc., and each member proceeds to act in pantomime in front of the audience. The game leader calls on individuals in the audience (with their hands raised) to guess the clues, words, etc., and eventually, the correct answer (in a predetermined amount of time). The acting team receives one point if they successfully got their message across. The teams exchange roles after each pantomime attempt.

I SAW

This is a fun variation of charades for the younger student (K-3rd grades). The game leader calls on one student to stand in front of the class and act in pantomime depicting an object or person he saw on his way to school. Before acting, the student should say "This morning, on my way to school, I saw..." (and then they start acting in pantomime). The actor then selects individuals (with their hands raised) in the audience to guess the correct answer. The student that finally guesses correctly is the next actor. The actors can give clues if the audience has a difficult time arriving at an answer.

GETTING WARMER & COLDER

WHERE TO PLAY: Classroom
NUMBER OF PLAYERS: 3 on up to a full classroom
SUGGESTED GRADE LEVELS: K-3rd grades
EQUIPMENT: A small object that can be easily hidden

Getting Warmer & Colder

HOW TO PLAY: One player is selected to be the searcher and leaves the room. The game leader chooses one player to hide a small object. The searcher is then called back into the room and immediately starts looking for the hidden object. The searcher can call on other players to help guide him closer and closer to the object. If the searcher is no where near the object, the players call out "Freezing." Then as the searcher gets closer, players can call out "cold," then"warm," and "hot.". The searcher is given one minute to find the object.

The game leader can use prizes or snacks (to serve as the object) to make finding the object even more exciting.

HOW MANY WORDS?

WHERE TO PLAY: Classroom
NUMBER OF PLAYERS: Two equally numbered groups
SUGGESTED GRADE LEVELS: K-4rd grades
EQUIPMENT: A clock or watch

HOW TO PLAY: One player from a team is chosen to call out a letter. His team has one minute to call out as many words as possible that begin with that letter. The game leader keeps count and monitors the time. At the conclusion of the time limit, the game leader tallies up the number of words. The opposing team then has their chance to come up with as many words as possible, in one minute, that begin with a certain letter (different from the first team). The team with the highest number of words wins.

HULA HOOP RELAY

WHERE TO PLAY: Classroom, or any large area
NUMBER OF PLAYERS: 6-12 players in each group; unlimited groups
SUGGESTED GRADE LEVELS: K-8th grades
EQUIPMENT: One hula hoop per group

HOW TO PLAY: Form evenly numbered circles, with each player holding hands with other circle players. Each circle starts the contest with one hula hoop (resting on the joined hands of two players).

On a starting signal, the players begin stepping through the hula hoop, with each group attempting to be the first one to bring the hula hoop around the circle and back to its starting place. Players are to keep their hands joined the entire time. Play several contests.

LIMBO

WHERE TO PLAY: In a room with an open space
NUMBER OF PLAYERS: An entire class
SUGGESTED GRADE LEVELS: K-8th grades
EQUIPMENT: One limbo stick; CD/tape player for music (optional)

HOW TO PLAY: This popular activity, in which children attempt to walk underneath a limbo stick without touching it, is best done to music. The game leader begins by selecting two players to hold the limbo stick about shoulder height. The other children form a line and, in turn, try to walk (facing upward) underneath the stick without touching it. A player is out if any part of his body touches the stick, or if he falls to the floor.

   After each round, select new limbo stick holders and adjust the limbo stick lower. Repeat this process with the stick getting lower and lower until only one player is left.

Limbo

MATHEMATICAL BASEBALL

WHERE TO PLAY: Indoors
NUMBER OF PLAYERS: Unlimited, although nine players on a team would be ideal.
GRADE LEVELS: 1st - 8th grades
EQUIPMENT: Bases, or objects to substitute for bases

HOW TO PLAY: First, design a baseball diamond by putting bases (about 6'- 8' apart). Divide the players into two equal teams. One team takes "fielding" positions –pitcher, catcher, etc. The other team lines up in a "batting" order.

The first batter steps up to home base. The pitcher calls out a mathematical problem–for example, "Five times Five equals what?" If the batter answers correctly, he is allowed to advance to first base. However, if the catcher answers correctly first, the batter is out.

Play continues in this fashion with batters either put out or advancing to first base. Any baserunners are also advanced if the batter answers correctly.

The pitcher may attempt to put out baserunners by calling out a problem their way. If the fielder at that base (first, second, third baseman) answers correctly before the baserunner, the baserunner is called out. If the baserunner answers first, he is allowed to advance to the next base.

Teams exchange sides after three outs, or when every batter has batted. The team with the highest number of runs after a predetermined number of innings wins the contest.

MUSICAL CHAIRS

WHERE TO PLAY: In a room that has the size to contain enough chairs needed to accommodate the number of participants.

NUMBER OF PLAYERS: 5 to 20 works best

GRADE LEVELS: K-6th grades

EQUIPMENT: One chair for each student except one: music (CD, tape, radio, etc.)

HOW TO PLAY: First, chairs needs to be placed in a straight line with every other chair facing in the opposite direction. For large groups, place the chairs back to back.

Musical Chairs

(continued on next page)

Musical Chairs (cont.)

Players are to begin by standing in a circle around the chair. At the sound of the music, they are to march in one direction circling the chairs. At any time, however, the game leader can turn off the music which is a signal to the players to find a seat as quickly as possible. The player left without a chair is eliminated from the game.

After each elimination, one chair is removed to keep the number of chairs one less than the number of players. Play continues in this fashion until a player wins the contest by capturing the last remaining chair.

NON-ELIMINATION MUSICAL CHAIRS

This version of Musical Chairs provides an alternative to the student elimination and one winner characteristics of regular Musical Chairs. In this activity, when the music stops, the players are to stand inside a hula hoop (or circles on the floor made with jump ropes) instead of sitting in a chair. The players can share a circle with others.

Before starting, the game leader needs to lay out a row of hula hoops (or circles made with jump ropes). The players move around the row of circles when the music plays, and when it stops, all the players move quickly to get at least one foot inside a circle. With each stoppage of the music, remove one of the circles to create more sharing of the remaining circles.

Non-Elimination Musical Chairs

PARTNER STEAL THE BACON

WHERE TO PLAY: Indoors or outdoors
NUMBER OF PLAYERS: Each player has a partner; unlimited pairs
SUGGESTED GRADE LEVELS: 1st-8th grades
EQUIPMENT: One beanbag for each pair of students

HOW TO PLAY: Have the paired players sit on the floor, legs crossed, facing each other. A beanbag is placed on the floor in the middle of the two players. The objective is to snatch the beanbag before the other player does, and at the same time, avoid being tagged on the arm/hand after grabbing it. The player snatching the bean bag should quickly place it between his crossed legs. Players are not allowed to stand or move about. The two players are to place their hands on their thighs before starting as a signal that each is "ready." One point is awarded to each player that successfully snatches the beanbag first without getting tagged on the arm or hand. A player can also get a point by tagging the player that grabbed the beanbag first (before he has deposited it between his legs). The first player to receive five points first wins. Rotate partners.

Partner Steal The Bacon

SCHOOLROOM TAG

WHERE TO PLAY: Classroom
NUMBER OF PLAYERS: An entire class
SUGGESTED GRADE LEVELS: K-3rd grades
EQUIPMENT: One long jump rope

HOW TO PLAY: With a long jump rope, make a circle on the floor in the front of the room.

(continued on next page)

Schoolroom Tag (cont.)

Assign one player to be the "It," and to stand near the circle. The leader calls out three or four names of his classmates and then yells out "Go." Each of the players called then attempt to be the first one to make it inside the circle without being tagged. The first player to do so becomes the new "It." Encourage the "Its" to call out different names so everyone has a chance at playing.

Schoolroom Tag

SILENT BALL

WHERE TO PLAY: In the classroom
NUMBER OF PLAYERS: An entire class
SUGGESTED GRADE LEVELS: 1st-8th grades
EQUIPMENT: Three foam balls

Silent Ball

(continued on next page)

Silent Ball (cont.)

HOW TO PLAY: Players are to sit on top of their desks. Three players are chosen to start with the foam balls. On a starting signal, the players begin tossing the balls around the room. Players can only toss a ball to players that have eye contact with them. If a player misses a pass, or throws an uncatchable pass, he is eliminated from the game and has to sit down. A player is also eliminated if he talked at any time. For maximum participation consider using two or more balls simultaneously.

SIMON SAYS

WHERE TO PLAY: Anywhere
NUMBER OF PLAYERS: Entire class
SUGGESTED GRADE LEVELS: K-4th grades
EQUIPMENT: None

HOW TO PLAY: One player is chosen to be the "Simon," and stands in front of the class. Simon issues a variety of commands while imitating the movements. However, the group only performs the movement if Simon has preceded the movement with the command, "Simon says." If the Simon says, "do this," or gives any other command besides "Simon says," the players are not to move. Those who move at the wrong time or perform an incorrect movement are eliminated from the game. The last player remaining becomes the next Simon.

To reduce student elimination time, consider playing several games simultaneously. This makes the game shorter and maximizes student participation.

Simon Says

NONELIMINATION SIMON SAYS

This is an interesting twist to the regular game of Simon Says. A player is chosen to be the "Simon." He stands in front of the class, and makes a statement and follows it with a command. An example would be, " If you walked to school this morning, touch your left elbow to someone's left elbow." If the statement is true about any of the players, they are to perform the movement; otherwise, players are not to move. The Simon can make any kind of informational statements– or completely offbeat ones just for the fun of it.

SPORTS DRAW

WHERE TO PLAY: Classroom (will need a chalkboard)
NUMBER OF PLAYERS: An entire class
SUGGESTED GRADE LEVELS: 2nd-6th grades
EQUIPMENT: Chalkboard; two pieces of chalk

HOW TO PLAY: This is a fun game that allows children to take turns drawing P.E. and sport related objects. Divide the class into two equal teams. Assign one player from each team to stand by the chalkboard.

Begin with the game leader whispering to each artist the name of a sport or physical education activity (basketball, football, etc.). The two artists will draw on the chalkboard an object that represents that particular activity. When finished, they call on teammates (who have their hand raised) to guess the correct answer. The first team to guess correctly is awarded one point. The artists cannot talk or give any clues.

Sports Draw

After each round, the game leader selects a different artist, giving them a specific sport or P.E. activity to draw. Continue in this fashion until every student has had a chance to draw. The team with the most points at the end wins.

WHERE'S MY MATES?

WHERE TO PLAY: Anywhere
NUMBER OF PLAYERS: An entire class
SUGGESTED GRADE LEVELS: K-6th grades
EQUIPMENT: Blindfolds (optional)

HOW TO PLAY: To begin, the game leader quietly whispers the name of an animal (dog, cat, horse, cow) in the ear of each player. The number of players with a particular animal should be equally numbered. The players then scatter, close their eyes (or wear blindfolds), and start making the distinctive sound of their assigned animal. The players are to move about, trying to hook up with others making the same sound. The first group to have all their "mates," wins the contest. Play again with different animals.

Where's My Mates?

WHO HAS THE TREASURE

WHERE TO PLAY: Anywhere
NUMBER OF PLAYERS: 6-10 in a group is ideal.
SUGGESTED GRADE LEVELS: K-3rd grades
EQUIPMENT: A coin (penny, nickel, etc.)

(continued on next page)

Who Has The Treasure(cont.)

HOW TO PLAY: Have the players sit closely together in a circle. One player is chosen to be the "hunter" and sits in the middle of the circle. The game leader will ask the hunter to close his eyes while one player in the circle is given a coin.

The game begins with the players passing the coin around the circle without showing the key, as the hunter watches. The players without the key (with their hands closed) pretend that they have the coin in order to keep the hunter guessing.

When the hunter suspects another player of having the coin, he calls out his name. The passing stops, and the player called upon reveals whether or not he has the coin. If this player has the coin, he becomes the next hunter. If not, the game continues.

Who Has The Treasure

CHAPTER SIX

GAMES USING ROPES, HOOPS & OTHER FUN STUFF!

Equipment such as parachutes, hula hoops, jump ropes, etc., add an exciting element to the school recess setting. Besides being challenging and fun, these activities can add tremendously to a child's overall level of physical fitness.

BEANBAG HORSESHOES

WHERE TO PLAY: Outside, either on grass or pavement
NUMBER OF PLAYERS: 2-4 players to a game; multiple games can be played simultaneously.
SUGGESTED GRADE LEVELS: 2nd-8th grades
EQUIPMENT: Two hula hoops (the smaller sizes); four beanbags per game

HOW TO PLAY: The traditional game of horseshoes is played, except that beanbags and hula hoops are used instead of the heavy, metal equipment normally used in regulation horseshoes. The hula hoops and beanbags offer a safer and more success-oriented setting for children.

Place two hula hoops about 15 to 30 feet apart as the targets. When throwing, players must stay behind the hoops. Each player is allowed two throws at a time. A beanbag that lands in the center of the hoop counts as 3 points, and a beanbag that ends up being the closest to a hoop (without a ringer being made) counts as 1 point. The first player (or team) to score 15 points is the game winner.

Beanbag Horseshoes

CROQUET

WHERE TO PLAY: Outside on a grass
NUMBER OF PLAYERS: Up to six players at a time; multiple games can be played if you have the equipment.
SUGGESTED GRADE LEVELS: 2nd-8th grades

EQUIPMENT: Six colored balls with a matching mallet for each player; nine wickets; two pegs.

HOW TO PLAY: Set up a playing course by placing the nine wickets evenly spaced apart in an hour-glass shaped formation. Before starting, players should decide a hitting order.

The first player sets his ball one mallet length in front of the stake and takes his shot. In order, the rest of the players do the same. Players are to move through the course counterclockwise, attempting to hit their ball through each wicket. A player earns a second stroke (called a continuation shot) each time he hits his ball through a wicket. Halfway through the course, each player must hit the opposite stake with his ball which also earns him a second stroke.

Whenever a player hits another player's ball, he earns two extra strokes. One of the two strokes can be used as a croquet shot. For the croquet shot, a player places his ball next to the opponent's ball (so that they are touching), puts his foot on his ball, and hits the side of his ball–sending the opponent's ball away. The opponent must play his ball from where it stops.

The first player to through the course and hit the starting stake wins. Play until everyone has finished.

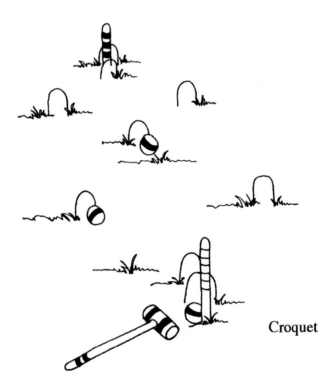

Croquet

MINIATURE CROQUET GOLF

This variation of croquet and golf is a fun alternative to regulation croquet. As the name of the game implies, this is actually miniature golf played with a croquet set. Three to six players to a course works best.

(continued on next page)

Minature Croquet Golf (cont.)

Set up a nine hole golf course with the wickets substituting for golf holes. Tape a number (one through nine) on each wicket.

To begin, the first player tees off by hitting the croquet ball toward the first hole (wicket #1). In order, the other players do the same. Continue until all the players have "holed-out." The player with the lowest score (that is, the fewest shots attempted to get the ball through the wicket) will tee-off first for the next hole.

The player completing the course in the fewest number of strokes is the winner.

Miniature Croquet Golf

BOCCE CROQUET

This game utilizes the skill of rolling (used in bocce) with croquet equipment. Set up the playing area by marking a bowling line that is 20-40 feet away from a row of wickets with a stake at the end. Three to six players to a course is an ideal number.

Bocce Croquet

The objective is to roll a ball from the bowling line, through all three wickets, hitting the stake. Players are to stay in a predetermined rolling order throughout the game. So that each player has a clear field to the stake, remove each previously rolled ball.

A player that hits the stake is awarded five points. A ball that goes through all three wickets but does not hit the stake is worth three points. A ball going through two wickets earns two points. A ball that makes it through one wicket is worth one point. The game winner is the first player to reach 15 points.

HULA HOOP CHALLENGES

The addition of hula hoops to the recess setting can present exciting and fun challenges for children. Below are a few challenges that game leaders will want to present to their students for non-stop excitement.

* Spin the hoop like a top or an eggbeater. Time how long you can make it spin. See how many times you can run around the hoop before it falls.

* Hula hoop around your waist, legs, neck, and arms. See how long can you keep it going. Try hula hooping with two or more hoops at the same time. See if you can switch arms while hula hooping.

* Use your hoop like a jump rope. Can you jump forward? Backwards? How many times can you jump without a mistake?

* Put a backward spin on the rope and make it roll back to you. How far can you throw it and still have it roll back to you?

(continued on next page)

Hula Hoop Challenges (cont.)

* See if you can roll your hoop forward and run through it while its still moving. See how many times you can shoot through back and forth before it falls.

* See if you can "Slip the Needle." Take a hoop that is on the ground and using only your feet, try to pick it up and kick it over your head.

HULA HOOP BUMPER TAG

WHERE TO PLAY: Anywhere
NUMBER OF PLAYERS: Two players to a hula hoop; unlimited groups
SUGGESTED GRADE LEVELS: K-6th grades
EQUIPMENT: One hula hoop for every two players; three foam balls

HOW TO PLAY: Divide the players into pairs; each pair stands inside a hoop and holds on waist high. Assign three groups to be the"Its." The "Its" start with one of the players holding a foam ball (to tag others with).

On a starting signal, the three "It" groups chase the others, attempting to tag either player inside a hula hoop. Any group that is tagged takes the ball and becomes the new "It" (therefore, the "Its" will be changing throughout the game). The groups that finish the game being the "It" the least often win.

Hula Hoop Bumper Tag

HULA HOOP CIRCLE RELAY

WHERE TO PLAY: Anywhere
NUMBER OF PLAYERS: 5-8 players to a circle; unlimited circles
SUGGESTED GRADE LEVELS: 1st-8th grades
EQUIPMENT: One hula hoop for each circle

HOW TO PLAY: Each group starts by holding hands in a circle. A hula hoop is placed between two players where it hangs from their joined hands. On a signal, they move the hoop around the circle, back to its starting spot, without letting go of the hands. Each team should raise their joined arms when finished. The team that finishes the relay and raises their arms first, wins the contest. Play several times.

Hula Hoop Circle Relay

LONG ROPE JUMPING CHALLENGES

The following tricks and challenges begin with the less difficult tasks which are aimed primarily for the younger and/or less experienced children. In order, they become progressively more difficult and challenging. Use ropes that are about 10 -12 feet long for kindergarten and first grade; 14 -16 feet for second graders and older students.

(continued on next page)

Long Rope Jumping Challenges (cont.)

Children need to be instructed in how to properly hold and turn a rope before beginning the challenges.

* Jump The Stick: The two turners hold the motionless rope so that the middle is about 6 inches off the floor. Jumpers take turns. Try doing 5-15 jumps without stopping. This is a good warm-up activity.

* High Water: Same as above except one turner holds the rope to the floor while the other turner holds it waist-high. Starting at the low end, the jumper progresses up the rope, jumping higher and higher as he approaches the high end of the rope.

* Pendulum Swing: The turners swing the rope back and forth like a clock pendulum (a half turn). Jumpers can either start in the middle or can run into the moving rope. Have jumpers attempt 10-20 consecutive jumps.

* Run Through: Turners execute the regular full swing of the rope. Players take turn running through the turning rope without getting touched by it.

* Regular Jumping: Jumpers attempt to jump a turning rope a predetermined number of times. Begin with jumpers starting in the middle. Progress to jumpers running into a turning rope to start.

* Stunts: Have the jumper attempt a variety of movements: quarter and half turns; touching the ground after each jump, straddle jumps, rocker steps, etc.

Also consider using equipment such as: bouncing a basketball while jumping; jumping with a short rope while in the middle; jumping a hula hoop (like a short rope) while in the middle; and juggling tennis balls while jumping in the middle.

* Hot Pepper: Turners begin by turning the rope slowly. They progressively turn it faster and faster while a player is jumping in the middle. See how many times each jumper will last.

* Rising Bridge: Turners start by turning the rope so that it hits the floor. After several turns of the rope, one of the two turners gradually walks backward causing the rope to rise higher and higher. Jumpers attempt to jump as high as possible without stopping the rope.

* Egg Beater: Two ropes are crossed in an "X" formation, each end held by a turner. In unison, one rope is turned clockwise with the other turned counterclockwise. The jumper enter the turning ropes, jumps 5-10 times, and exits without stopping the rope.

* Double-Dutch: This stunt involves two ropes being turned alternately toward each other. Have the players spend plenty of time perfecting the turn before allowing jumpers. Remind the jumpers to focus on the rope furthermost away and to enter as it nears the floor.

Jump Rope rhymes are very popular and can help children keep rhythm, keep jump counts, and describe stunts to be performed. Here are a few:

1. (Jump Counting) *Candy, candy in the dish:*
How many pieces do you wish?
One, Two, Three (and so on).

2. (Jump Counting) *Tick Tock, Tick Tock,*
Give the time by the clock.
It's one, two, (up to midnight).

3. (Jump Counting) *James, James (student's name) at the gate,*
Eating cherries from a plate.
How many cherries did he eat?
One, Two, Three (and so on).

4. (Jump Counting) *Alphabet, alphabet,*
I know my A, B, C's
Alphabet, alphabet,
Listen to me...A, B, C (all the way to Z)

5. (Stunt Performing) *Teddy Bear, Teddy Bear, turn around,*
Teddy Bear, Teddy Bear, touch the ground,
Teddy Bear, Teddy Bear, touch your shoe,
Teddy Bear, Teddy Bear, jump turn, too
Teddy Bear, Teddy Bear, go upstairs (lift knees high)
Teddy Bear, Teddy Bear, say your prayers,
Teddy Bear, Teddy Bear, turn out the light,
Teddy Bear, Teddy Bear, say good night (jumper exits).

6. (Hot Pepper) *James, James (student's name), set the table,*
bring the plates if you are able.
Don't forget the salt and
the red hot pepper (turners turn the rope faster and faster).

7. (Hot Pepper)

I like milk, I like tea,
How many girls (boys) are wild about me?
One, Two, (and so on as the rope turns faster and faster)

PARACHUTE CHALLENGES

Parachute play brings a new level of excitement to any school setting and can be enjoyed by children of all ages. One of the larger parachute can usually accommodate up to 25-30 players at one time. Besides game activities, children enjoy challenges put forth such as the following.

POPCORN

Place foam or whiffle balls on the parachute. Have the players shake the parachute as vigorously as possible in order for the balls to "pop" out.

Popcorn

CLEAN THE CHUTE

Have the players jump up and down, and shake the parachute as vigorously possible in order to "clean the chute." A great warm-up activity.

(continued on next page)

Clean The Chute

DOME

Have the players start with one knee on the ground along with the parachute. On a signal, the players quickly stand up, raise the parachute above their heads and then return to their starting position. This traps the air under the chute creating the "dome" effect.

Dome

MERRY GO ROUND

The players are to hold on with one hand (all with the same hand) and perform different locomotor movements (running, skipping, galloping, etc.) as they circle either clockwise or counterclockwise.

Merry Go Round

NUMBER EXCHANGE

Have the players count off by fours. The game leader calls out a number as a dome (see above) is being made. Those players with the called number must exchange positions with each other before the chute comes back to the ground.

Number Exchange

IGLOO

Have the players raise the parachute upward as they walk forward three steps. After the third step, the players turn, regrasp the edge of the chute, and sit on the floor with their bottoms on the edge of the parachute. All of the players should now be sitting inside their "igloo."

Igloo

POISONOUS SNAKES

Place some short jump ropes on the parachute. Players begin shaking the parachute, attempting to shake all the "poisonous snakes" off the chute. However, warn players to avoid having a rope touch them (a "snake bite") or else they will have to run to the nearest wall and back (to get rid of the poison) before being allowed to play again.

Poisonous Snakes

THE SHARK

The players inflate the parachute, take two steps forward, and then let go of the chute. The chute will float briefly, but eventually land somewhere in the playing area. Players pretend the chute is "shark" and run to the closest wall to escape being gobbled up.

The Shark

PARACHUTE VOLLEYBALL

WHERE TO PLAY: Anywhere
NUMBER OF PLAYERS: An entire class
SUGGESTED GRADE LEVELS: 2nd-8th grades
EQUIPMENT: One parachute; one volleyball

HOW TO PLAY: The players are divided into two equal teams who stand on opposite sides of the parachute facing each other. Place a volleyball in the middle of the parachute.

(continued on next page)

Parachute Volleyball

On a starting signal, each team tries to shake the volleyball off the chute over the heads of their opponents. A team scores one point for each successful "spike." Play to 15 points.

PARACHUTE GOLF

WHERE TO PLAY: Anywhere
NUMBER OF PLAYERS: An entire class
SUGGESTED GRADE LEVELS: 2nd-8th grades
EQUIPMENT: One parachute; two different colored plastic balls

HOW TO PLAY: The players are divided into two equal teams who stand on opposite sides of the parachute facing each other. Each team is assigned a "golf ball" that is a certain color; both balls are put on the parachute.

On a starting signal, each team tries to shake and roll their ball into the center hole of the chute and, at the same time, prevent the other team from putting its ball through the center hole. A team receives one point each time its ball goes through the hole. Play for a predetermined time period.

Parachute Golf

PARACHUTE STEAL THE BACON

WHERE TO PLAY: Anywhere
NUMBER OF PLAYERS: An entire class
SUGGESTED GRADE LEVELS: 1st-8th grades
EQUIPMENT: One parachute; one beanbag

HOW TO PLAY: Divide the players into two equal teams with each team facing inward on opposite sides of the parachute. Place one beanbag on the floor underneath the parachute. Assign a number to each team member.

On a signal, the players raise the parachute. At the same time, the game leader calls out a number. The two players with that number run underneath the chute, each trying to grab the beanbag before the other. The player grabbing the beanbag must return to his position without the opponent tagging him first.

A player can earn one point for his team by grabbing the beanbag and returning to his position without being tagged. A point can also be earned by tagging a player who has the beanbag before he was able to get back in his position. No points are earned if the parachute falls on the player with the beanbag.

Play for a predetermined time or point total.

Parachute Steal The Bacon

SHORT ROPE CHALLENGES

The following rope challenges begin with the less difficult tasks which are primarily for the younger and less experienced jumper. In order, the challenges become progressively more difficult. Use ropes that are of appropriate lengths. Most K-2nd graders will use 5-6 foot ropes, 3rd-4th graders will want 6-7 foot ropes, and the older students will want 8-9 foot ropes.

Children need to be properly instructed on how to hold and turn a rope before beginning most of these challenges.

* Double Jump: Player jumps twice, off both feet, for every turn of the rope; once when the rope is overhead and again as it passes underneath the feet.

* Single Jump: Player jumps once, off both feet, for every turn of the rope.

* Backward Swing: Using either the double jump or single jump, turn the rope backwards and try jumping.

* Jogging (Or Alternate Foot) Step: Using a running pattern, alternate landing on the right foot, and then left foot as the rope passes underneath.

* Boxer: Jump twice on the right foot, then twice on the left foot. Continue jumping twice on each foot.

* Rocker: Start with one foot forward. As the rope passes under the front foot, shift the weight from the back foot to the front foot (lifting the back foot up).Shift weight from the front foot to the back foot after the rope passes underneath.

* Side Swing & Jump: Swing the rope, held with both hands, to one side of the body and then the other. After the two side swings, jump once, off both feet. Repeat the swing-swing-jump pattern.

* Side Straddle: Start with both feet together. On the first turn, jump with legs shoulder-width apart. On the second turn, bring legs back together. Repeat the together-apart-together pattern (much as the footwork in a jumping jack).

* Mountain Climber: Start in a stride position with one leg in front of the other. As the rope passes underneath, the jumper jumps into the air and reverses the position of the feet.

* Skier: Jump sideways, off both feet, over a line on the floor. The sideways motion is similar to how skiers move down a mountain slope.

* Cross Legs Jump (or "X" Jump): The player begins by jumping, off both feet, sideways apart. On the second turn, he jumps with the right foot in front of the left. On the third turn of the rope, he straddles feet apart. On the fourth turn, he crosses the left foot in front of the right. Repeat the pattern.

(continued on next page)

Short Rope Challenges (cont.)

* Heel-to-Heel: On the first turn of the rope, touch the right heel to the floor. Switch heels on the second turn. Repeat the right-left-right-left pattern.

* Heel-to-Toe: On the first turn, the jumper touches his right heel to the floor. On the second turn, he touches his right toe next to his left foot. He then repeats this same pattern with his left foot.

* Forward Criss-Cross: Start with feet together. As the rope is turning overhead, cross the arms creating a loop. Jump through the loop, uncross the arms and single jump. As the rope turns overhead, cross the arms again. Repeat the pattern.

* Backward Criss-Cross: Same as above except the rope is turned backwards.

* Double-Unders: The objective is to turn the rope twice for every jump. To be successful, a jumper will need to jump higher off the floor and bend slightly at the waist. Whip the wrists quickly to make the rope rotate faster.

TEAM TUG-OF-WAR

WHERE TO PLAY: Outside on grass
NUMBER OF PLAYERS: Unlimited
SUGGESTED GRADE LEVELS: 1st-8th grades
EQUIPMENT: Two or more tug-of-war ropes

HOW TO PLAY: Place two or more tug-of-war ropes parallel to each other about 15-20 feet apart. The middle of each rope should lie across a line marking. Depending on the number of ropes available, divide the players into equal teams.

On a signal, all the teams begin pulling. A team wins if it can pull the other team across the line marking. After each contest rotate the teams. When each team has challenged each other, tally up the number of wins. The team with the highest number of wins is declared the champion for the event.

Team Tug-Of-War

INDEX

ALPHABETICAL LISTING OF GAMES

(continued on next page)

Index (cont.)

ABOUT THE AUTHOR

Guy Bailey, MEd, is an elementary physical education specialist for the Evergreen School District in Vancouver, Washington. Guy has over twenty years of experience teaching K-8 grade physical education. During this time, he has also coached numerous youth sports and intramural activities. He received his Bachelor's degree from Central Washington University and his Master's degree from Portland State University.

In addition to this book, Guy has also authored *The Ultimate Sport Lead-Up Game Book*. It is widely considered the most complete and comprehensive resource on the subject of sport lead-up games for K-8 grade children.

Guy's professional goal is to equip each of his students with a love of movement and the basic skills needed to participate in an active lifestyle now and as adults. He believes that for long-lasting skill development to take place, physical education needs to consist of success-oriented learning experiences that literally leave students craving more. Both this book and *The Ultimate Sport Lead-Up Game Book* reflect Guy's philosophy of using skill-based activities that are fun, exciting, and meaningful.

In his spare time, Guy enjoys jogging, weightlifting, hiking, and fishing the beautiful Columbia River near his home town of Camas, WA. He also has a passion for college athletics and is a frequent visitor to PAC-10 stadiums and gymnasiums throughout the Pacific Northwest.

Guy is an active member of the *American Alliance Of Health, Physical Education, Recreation and Dance*.

EDUCATORS PRESS
INFORMATION & BOOK REQUEST

To order additional copies of *The Ultimate Playground & Recess Game Book*, please contact your favorite bookstore or catalog company. You can also order directly from the publisher. Call (360) 834-3049 or write to the publisher's address listed below to order by check. For faster processing and/or credit card purchases please call toll-free:

1-800-431-1579

This book, as well as *The Ultimate Sport Lead-Up Game Book*, is available at quantity discounts. Contact the publisher for more information.

Educators Press
5333 NW Jackson St.
Camas, WA 98607
(360) 834-3049